D1125448

A Kilo of String

Rob Johnson

XERIKA PUBLISHING

A KILO OF STRING

Published by Xerika Publishing

Copyright © Rob Johnson 2017

In order to maintain their anonymity, the names of individuals and places have been changed in some instances. Some identifying characteristics and details may also have been changed, such as physical properties, occupations and places of residence.

Cover design by Penny Philcox.

First published 2017 by Xerika Publishing
10 The Croft, Bamford, Hope Valley,
Derbyshire S33 0AP

ISBN: 978-0-9926384-8-1

http://www.rob-johnson.org.uk

For all our Greek friends who have made us feel so welcome here and for all the people of Greece who have suffered so much during these times of austerity.

ACKNOWLEDGEMENTS

I am indebted to the following people for helping to make this book better than it would have been without their advice, technical knowhow and support:

Yannis Anagnopoulos; Nuala Forde; Dan Varndell; Chris Wallbridge; Cynthia Wallbridge; Nick Whitton; Patrick and Heidi Woodgate.

Many thanks also to the people of Greece, who have made us feel so welcome here, and to everyone who has provided me with material for this book – either knowingly or unknowingly.

And finally, my eternal gratitude to my wife, Penny, for her unfailing support, encouragement and belief, even though she disputes several of the things I've said in this book and still insists I did a happy dance when she accepted my marriage proposal. As if!

COVER DESIGN BY PENNY PHILCOX

Special thanks as always to Penny Philcox for the original artwork for the cover. I hope I didn't drive you quite as mad with this one as I did with the previous one.

GREEK LANGUAGE NOTE

There are a few Greek words and phrases used in the text, and these have been transliterated into the Latin alphabet. Where a word has more than one syllable, an accent shows which is the stressed syllable. For instance, the Greek word *póso* (meaning "how much") is pronounced with the stress on the first "o".

The letter "i" has no dot above it in Greek and is written "ι".

When you address someone directly by name in Greek and their name ends in an "s", the "s" is omitted. For instance, a man called Dimitris would be addressed as Dimitri. For the sake of simplicity, however, this rule has not been observed in the text.

'A KILO OF STRING' PODCAST SERIES

Some of the material in *A Kilo of String* is loosely based on Rob Johnson's podcast series of the same name. All episodes are free to listen to and download at:
https://rob-johnson.org.uk/podcasts/a-kilo-of-string/

CONTENTS

NOT REALLY A PREFACE

(People tend to skip prefaces)

How Greek Was My Valley. That's what I was going to call this book because I rather liked the play on words in reference to the 1941 film, *How Green Was My Valley*. However, there were two main reasons why I eventually decided against it:

- We don't live in a valley at all, so I really can't claim it as *mine* or have any idea how Greek it may or may not be. On the contrary, we live halfway up a mountain, and since it's very definitely a Greek mountain, there didn't seem to be much point in speculating about its Greekness.

- The film, *How Green Was My Valley* (and the novel that it's based on), is about a coal mining community in South Wales, and I didn't want to mislead anyone into believing that this was a book about coal mining in Greece – which it very definitely isn't.

In the interests of accuracy, I suppose I could have called the book *How Greek Was the Place Where We Live That's Halfway Up a Mountain*, but it didn't strike me as particularly catchy as a title. *Driving Over Olives* had a rather nice ring to it but was perhaps a little too derivative, so in the end I went with *A Kilo of String* which, coincidentally, is the title of my podcast series about some of our experiences since moving to Greece.

And why did I call the podcast series *A Kilo of String*?

Because it comes from an incident that epitomises many of the things that have seemed bizarre to my partner (now wife) Penny and I during the thirteen years we've lived here. I certainly wouldn't have expected that our first encounter with culture shock would be over something as apparently straightforward as buying rope or string, but that's exactly how it came about.

In Greece, they don't tend to go in for the B&Q-type DIY megastores except in the bigger towns and cities. Instead, they've stuck more with the traditional style of shops such as the kind of hardware stores that used to be on every British high street until about the 1980s. The first time I went into one of these places, I wanted to buy some rope, so I found a display rack which had several different thicknesses of rope and string on individual spools.

'I'd like some rope, please,' I said to the shopkeeper in a rough approximation of Greek, having previously looked up the words in our pocket dictionary.

'*Málısta. Poıó thélate?*'

I was fairly sure he was asking me which sort I wanted, so I pointed to the appropriate spool.

'*Entáxeı. Pósa kılá tha thélate?*' said the shopkeeper.

The question totally floored me. Primitive though my knowledge of Greek was at that stage, it sounded a lot like he was asking me how many kilos I wanted. He'd obviously misunderstood me, so I patted the spool and gave it a sideways nod for emphasis.

'Yes, I know,' he said in English and with more than a hint of impatience in his tone. 'But how many *kilos*?'

This was getting ridiculous. How should I know how many kilos?

'I've no idea,' I said. 'I just want ten metres.'

'Okay,' said the shopkeeper and waved me aside before reeling off some of the rope, using his arms as a measure until he'd got about ten metres' worth. Then he cut it off, took it to the counter, weighed it and charged me at the rate per kilo.

As far as we or anybody else can work out, there doesn't seem to be any particular logic for selling things like rope, string, wine, olive oil and even bubblewrap by the kilo. If you ask a Greek, more often than not they'll just shrug and say they've always done it like that so what's the problem? Well, it isn't a problem at all once you get used to it or the multitude of other examples in Greece for which there doesn't appear to be any logical reason.

In supermarkets, for instance, you'll often find a free gift taped to a particular product even though the two items bear no relation to each other whatsoever. Take a jumbo-sized pack of washing powder. What's the free gift? Bottle of fabric conditioner? Some other household cleaning aid perhaps? No, it's a can of Coke or a packet of crisps. So where's the logic in that? Okay, you might be able to make a case based on people getting hungry and/or thirsty when they're doing the weekly wash, but it's a bit on the tenuous side, isn't it?

In Greece, you just have to accept that there aren't any logical explanations for a lot of the weird stuff you come across here, which has always struck me as rather ironic considering it was the Greeks who pretty much invented logic – the word itself coming from the original Greek *logikí*. But maybe that was so long ago that they eventually became bored with it and decided to do chaos instead, which is of course another Greek invention, "chaos" coming, oddly enough, from the Greek word *cháos*.

And in case I'm beginning to sound like the stereotypical British expat who's constantly moaning on about the perceived shortcomings of whatever country it is that they've chosen to settle in, I'd be the first to admit that we Brits aren't exactly innocent when it comes to weirdness. Apologising to the person who's just run over *your* foot with *their* shopping trolley, believing that tea will cure almost anything from a broken heart to a broken leg, obsessive compulsive queuing disorder, and spending entire weekends on a freezing cold station platform jotting down train numbers are only a few examples.

But because I've grown up with these kinds of weirdness, I don't find them weird at all – except the trainspotting one, obviously – and it's only when a non-Brit points them out that I can begin to understand that they might not be universally acknowledged as perfectly normal. By the same token, it's purely because I'm a foreigner in Greece that certain aspects of the Greek way of life strike me as odd or even downright weird, whereas a Greek would find them as natural as selling string by the kilo.

When Penny and I moved here in early 2004, our most overused word for the first few weeks was "bizarre", and you'll find many reasons for this through the pages of this book. Hopefully, however, you'll also discover why it is that we're still here thirteen years later and have no intention of leaving unless some major catastrophe occurs, which, knowing my luck and the way European and global events have been going lately, it probably will.

What you definitely won't find out is anything at all about a Greek valley – mine or anybody else's – and therefore no indication whatsoever whether it's green or some other colour of the spectrum. Sorry about that.

1

Haemorrhaging Away

I'd like to make it clear right here and now that neither Penny nor I are completely insane. In fact, Penny is a fully qualified psychological counsellor, so she should know, right? There were, however, quite a few people who thought we were – to use a technical term – stark staring bonkers when we first announced our intention to move to Greece.

Maybe they'd been watching too many of the various "Brits moving abroad" series on TV where, in almost every programme, the narrator would say, 'But they soon discovered that their savings were haemorrhaging away.' Not dwindling or seeping, but *haemorrhaging*. The line was always delivered in the hushed tone of a David Attenborough crawling around in the jungle and describing the mating habits of a bunch of silverback gorillas, and it scared the hell out of us every time we heard it.

In almost every episode, somebody's savings were haemorrhaging away, and it could easily have put us off the whole idea of moving abroad except for one thing. An awful lot of the people they filmed for these programmes seemed to have about as much idea of a sound business proposal as whoever invented the inflatable dartboard or the helicopter ejector seat.

Take Mr and Mrs X, for example. They'd sold their house, cashed in all their life assurance policies and bought some dilapidated hotel that they were going to turn into a winter sports centre and run skiing holidays. But here's the part which seems to indicate that they hadn't really thought things through properly. It was in Benidorm.

Actually, I made that bit up, but seriously, they were planning to do the whole Swiss chalet thing on such a tight budget that all they had left in the bank for "emergencies" was about five hundred quid.

Anyway, sure enough, they had all kinds of emergencies, unforeseen expenses and whatnot which, to be honest, would have been easily foreseen by every single viewer watching the programme. So it didn't exactly come as a huge surprise to anyone except Mr and Mrs X that their money was "haemorrhaging away".

While I'm on the subject, the production company responsible for one of these Brits-moving-abroad TV shows approached a couple of friends of ours who were in the process of doing exactly that and asked them if they'd be interested in participating. But it soon became clear from the researcher's questions that they were actively looking for people who were likely to fail. You can hardly blame them, I suppose. Failures, cockups and money haemorrhaging away makes for far more interesting telly than when everything goes smoothly.

When we were in the early stages of making our own arrangements to move to Greece, somebody asked us what *we'd* do if we were invited to be in one of these shows, and we said we'd freak out if we applied and got accepted. Why? Because it would mean that the production company had spotted a serious flaw in our plans which we hadn't foreseen ourselves and which would inevitably lead to the whole haemorrhaging away scenario.

On the contrary, our plans – or so we hoped – had been meticulously laid, and our preparations had begun

16

about a year before the big move itself. The first thing we decided to do was to take a fortnight's holiday in Greece to try and get an idea of the kind of area we wanted to move *to*. This in itself presented us with our very first hurdle as I hadn't been on an aeroplane in over twenty years and, to put it mildly, wasn't overly keen to repeat the experience.

My main problem with flying isn't that I think the plane is suddenly going to plummet to the ground for no apparent reason – or even a perfectly logical reason. I know all the statistics about how flying is supposed to be the safest form of transport and that you're more likely to be eaten by a pterodactyl than die in a plane crash. It's just that I hate the idea of being locked inside a metal tube for hours without any means of escape. At least on a train there's an emergency communication cord you can pull when you've decided you've had enough and want to get off. There'd be a hefty fine which I'd be reluctant to pay, of course, but I take some comfort in knowing that a way out is available if the claustrophobia got too overwhelming.

The last time I even *contemplated* getting on a plane was when I had the opportunity to visit some friends in Russia, and flying seemed to be the only feasible way to get there. So, I went to see my doctor to ask if there was anything he could prescribe – something along the lines of a long-acting horse tranquiliser. But when I told him about my terror of flying, he said, 'Oh yes, I know. I'm exactly the same.' Then he went on to tell me how his worst ever moment on a plane was when he'd had to go to the toilet, and as he sat there, he looked down at the floor between his feet and thought, 'God, all that's between me and the ground is thirty thousand feet of fresh air and this piece of metal.' He wrote me a prescription for beta blockers, which didn't seem to have any effect at all, so I never did get to Russia.

But back to the impending threat of having to get on a plane to Greece...

'Well, why don't we take it one step at a time and do a short flight somewhere else first?' said Penny. 'Ireland maybe.'

This seemed like the perfect solution in theory, but the proof of the pudding was in the sheer terror I experienced during even that short hop across the Irish Sea. What I hadn't taken into account is that the shorter the flight is, the smaller the plane, and every slight gust of wind and mechanical "clunk" is amplified several times over. Somewhat foolishly in hindsight, we'd also chosen to sit as close to the middle of the plane as possible, which unfortunately turned out to be directly above the landing gear. "Unfortunately" because when the wheels were retracted soon after takeoff, this particular "clunk" came from directly under my seat and felt like the whole plane was about to split in two.

To be perfectly honest, Penny hadn't been much help either.

'I'll be right next to you the whole time,' she'd said when she'd first persuaded me to get on the big iron bird in sky. 'And after all, I *am* a fully qualified psychological therapist.'

This had certainly been reassuring until the moment we'd boarded the plane and were sitting on the runway, waiting for the inevitable roar of the engines which would announce our imminent and wholly unnatural departure from *terra firma*. My knuckles were already ivory white from gripping the armrests of my aisle seat, and I stared directly ahead, desperately trying to imagine I was on a train. Penny was next to me in the window seat, gazing at the outside world and taking not the slightest notice of my rapidly mounting anxiety.

'Er, Penny,' I said through teeth clenched as tightly as whatever animal it is that you have to break their jaws to

18

make them let go when they bite you. 'I'm really struggling with this.'

There was no response, so I slowly pivoted my head towards her and placed my hand on her arm. 'Are you listening to me? I said I'm really struggling here.'

It was at this point that she turned to face me and removed one of her earplugs. 'Sorry, what did you say?'

And I always thought that one of the most important qualities in a psychological therapist was the ability to *listen*.

Not long after this and the landing gear trauma, I was still staring fixedly ahead and trying to imagine I was on a train when she said, 'Oh look, that's Anglesey down there.'

When it came to the flight home, I decided I ought to get used to the idea of being airborne since we'd already booked the Greece flights, and they'd be more like four hours instead of the current thirty minutes. Consequently, I dispensed with the "I'm-on-a-train, I'm-on-a-train" mental mantra and tried to convince myself that being thirty thousand feet up in the air was perfectly natural and not really terrifying at all.

I hadn't actually communicated this new strategy to Penny, however, so when she looked horizontally out of the window and said, 'Oh look, we're just going through Anglesey Station', it was with the best of intentions.

'Oh my God! We've crashed!' I shrieked, and I braced myself for the impact.

We did eventually make it safely back to Planet Earth, and a couple of weeks later we were boarding the plane to Greece. During the intervening period, I'd read almost everything there was to read on the subject of "How To Avoid Completely Freaking Out On Aeroplanes", and one tip I picked up was that you should tell one of the stewards that you're a nervous flier as soon as you get on the plane. So that's what I did. Not that it seemed to make the slightest difference though. I didn't notice any of the cabin crew keeping a particular eye on me or coming to offer me soothing words of reassurance every few minutes. As far as I could tell, the only difference it *did* make was when I was hurrying towards the exit door after we'd landed, and the steward I'd spoken to when I'd first got on the plane gave me a beaming smile and said, 'You made it then.'

I spent the next fortnight trying not to think about the flight home and concentrate instead on the job in hand – checking out the area we were staying in to see if it was the part of Greece where we might want to live. We were in a village called Agios Nikolaos, which is near to Stoupa on the Mani peninsula, and if you know anything at all about the shape of Greece, there are three long pointy bits sticking out at the bottom and the Mani is the middle one.

We did quite a lot of exploring, and in many ways it was the perfect location, location, location. Amazing scenery, dramatic mountains, great beaches, etcetera, all of which were very appealing except for a couple of fairly major drawbacks. Stoupa and its fairly immediate surroundings are very much a tourist hotspot, which means that the place is heaving with holidaymakers during the summer. For the rest of the year, there's hardly a shop or taverna that stays open, and the area is almost entirely deserted apart from a few expats, most of whom are British. We'd no intention of moving to Greece just to become part of some British expat enclave, and we probably wouldn't have been accepted anyway because we're not that keen on gin and tonic and neither of us has got the faintest clue how to play bridge.

By the time we'd come to the conclusion that the Stoupa area wasn't for us, it was too late to do any exploring further afield, and we realised that there was nothing for it but to go back to England and begin the serious process of biting bullets, upping sticks and burning some bridges. (There may have been some other metaphors – appropriate or otherwise – but I can't remember what they were now.)

2

Roses Are Red, Ferraris Are Blue

So there we were, back in good old Blighty, having made the decision (bitten the bullet) that we'd sell up (burn our bridges) and move (up sticks) to Greece even though we hadn't yet found anywhere to move *to*.

Of the many other metaphors which sprang to mind at the time was "You can't fit a quart into a pint pot". (For the benefit of younger readers, this would translate loosely as "You can't fit a litre into a half-litre pot", which, in my opinion, isn't an expression that's likely to catch on.) This was a problem that became disturbingly evident once we'd arranged for a forty foot container to transport our furniture and other goods and chattels to Athens, where they would stay until we'd found somewhere to live. Consequently, we now had to get rid of about an eighty foot container's worth of stuff which there wouldn't be room for.

This involved several trips to a variety of charity shops, but we also thought that some of the bits and pieces we were discarding might be worth a few bob, so we got in touch with the local auctioneers. They sent someone round the next day, but he clearly had a very different idea to us about what was a valuable antique and what was worthless junk.

'What about this table?' I said. 'It's been in my family for generations,' I lied. 'An antiques dealer once offered my parents three hundred quid for it, and that was thirty years ago.' (This last bit was true.)

'Ah yes,' said the auctioneer with a scratch of his chin, 'but tastes have changed since then, I'm afraid.'

'Oh really?' I said. 'You mean people don't like tables any more?'

He ignored my question, but I ploughed on with another one. 'And what happens when people eventually wake up to the realisation that Louis Quinze furniture is ridiculously ornate and really rather ugly – not to mention bloody uncomfortable? All of a sudden it's worthless?'

The auctioneer ignored me once again and turned his attention to my prized collection of Dinky, Corgi and Matchbox toy cars and half a dozen Action Men (complete with a vast array of outfits and weaponry and most of them in full possession of all four of their limbs).

'Now these have got to be worth something surely,' I said.

The auctioneer picked up one of my all-time favourite Dinky toys – a bright blue, single-seater Ferrari racing car – and turned it this way and that in his hand with what appeared to be the beginnings of a sneer.

'It's not exactly what you'd call "pristine", is it?'

'Pristine?' I said, failing to control my mounting indignation.

'Pristine. It means "in its original condition".'

'Yes, I do know what pristine means.'

'For a start, I've never seen a Ferrari in this particular shade of blue before.'

'It got bashed about a bit,' I said, 'so my brother repainted it.'

'As presumably he did with the orange and purple Rolls Royce Silver Shadow,' said the auctioneer with a disdainful nod at the pile of toy cars on the floor.

'The thing is,' he went on, returning the Ferrari to the heap and wiping the lenses of his half-moon glasses on a neatly pressed handkerchief, 'this sort of thing is only worth anything if it's in immaculate condition and preferably still in its original box.'

Okay, this wasn't exactly news to me, but I've always been amazed at how any toy could survive the decades so perfectly and why it would still be in its box. You'd definitely have to question the state of mind of the kid it was given to in the first place:

> *'I say, father, thank you very much. I'll just pop it up here on the shelf with all my other still-boxed toys and it'll be worth a lot of money when I'm seventy.'*
>
> *'That's the spirit. Good man, Tarquin.'*

By now, the auctioneer had picked up Sergeant Troy Stone, the fearless veteran of many an Action Man battle, and his distaste this time was totally undisguised.

'I mean, look at this,' he said. 'It hasn't even got a face.'

I gave the kind of pouty shrug I'd begun to master when I'd been told off by my dad at about the age I was when I first started playing with Action Men.

'He got burned,' I mumbled. 'Flamethrower attack.'

The auctioneer was obviously unimpressed by Sergeant Stone's heroic exploits and dropped him unceremoniously back with his plastic and vinyl comrades-in-arms.

Suffice it to say, we made very little from the sale of the precious items which eventually got sold at auction, but I did keep back a few of my favourite Dinky and Corgi toys such as my James Bond Aston Martin with the ejector seat and the *Man From UNCLE* car where Napoleon Solo and Illya Kuryakin take it in turns to fire their guns out of the side windows when you press a button on the top. As for my loyal band of Action Men, well I just couldn't bring myself to part with them in the end, could I?

Something else which I couldn't bear to part with was a single one of my rather large collection of books. Penny had other ideas and insisted – no, *demanded* – that I shed at least a third of them.

'Why don't you sort them into three piles?' she suggested. 'One for definitely keeping, one for definitely not keeping, and one for undecided.'

Well, I did my best to comply – honest I did – but it was an almost impossible task, and Penny was less than impressed when she came to inspect the three stacks of books when I'd finished. I say "stacks", although I have to admit that this was somewhat of an overstatement in two of the three cases.

'I presume these two books aren't the "definitely keeping" pile,' she said.

'No,' I said with more than a hint of pride. 'They're the ones that are definitely going to Oxfam.'

'And what about these four?'

'Undecided.'

She then randomly selected one of the books from the "definitely keeping" pile.

'A Haynes Manual for a 1970 to 79 Vauxhall Viva?'

'It was the first car I ever owned,' I said. 'Besides, it'll come in handy if we ever have another Vauxhall Viva in the future.'

'1970 to 79.'

'Quite.'

I did actually win the argument over this particular volume on the basis of its practical and sentimental value, but this was sadly not true of the four or five large boxes of other books from my "definitely keeping" pile. Penny insists that this is a gross exaggeration and that it was a single, medium-sized boxful, but however many boxes it was, I still had to dispense with far more books than I considered reasonable. This was after I'd failed to convince Penny that there'd be a lot more room for my books if she binned some of the pieces of "art" her kids had made at school many years ago. Perhaps not surprisingly, this suggestion didn't go down at all well, especially after I'd picked up one of the many amorphous blobs of glazed clay and said, 'I mean, what on earth is this supposed to be?'

Up until that point, I could never have imagined that anyone could pack quite so much venom into the simple phrase, "It's a tortoise".

The *entente cordiale* between us having been somewhat weakened by now, it received a further blow the following day when I was putting something into one of the black plastic sacks that was clearly destined for the rubbish tip. In amongst the rest of the landfill fodder, I discovered not one but three books, all of which seemed to be in perfectly good condition.

'They're my books, so I can do what I like with them,' Penny said after I'd fished them out and asked her why she'd dumped them in the rubbish sack.

'Fair enough,' I said, 'but you could at least have put them in the recycling bag. Better still, why not give them to one of the charity shops?'

'Oh yes?' she said, snatching one of the three books out of my hand. 'And who's going to want a 1962 book about the human anatomy?'

'Well, I'm by no means a medical man by any stretch of the imagination, but as far as I'm aware, the human anatomy hasn't really changed very much in the last forty years.'

As I recall, the "discussion" got a little out of hand after that, possibly because I may have made some passing reference to book-burners and Adolf Hitler. This also probably explains why I later discovered a dozen pairs of my underpants in the rubbish sack when there was still plenty of wear left in them, not to mention quite a few good-sized ventilation holes. Hell hath no fury like a woman who you've just accused of being a Nazi book-burner.

3

Pompeii and Circumstance

The *entente cordiale* having eventually been restored between us, and after numerous selfless compromises on my part, Penny and I managed to whittle down our worldly possessions to what we were pretty sure would fit into a forty foot container – with a bit left over to be taken with us in the camper van. – No, not "a bit" – a *lot*. We'd no idea how long it would be before we found a place to live in Greece, so we had to take everything with us that we might need over the next few weeks or even months.

By now, we were almost ready to hit the open road, but to make sure we hadn't forgotten something crucial, I thought it would be a good idea to double-check the questionnaire in one of the dozens of books we'd read on the subject of moving abroad. This one was called *Going to Live In Greece: Your Practical Guide to Life and Work in Greece* by Peter Reynolds (2003), and the questionnaire appeared in a chapter called *Getting There*. Here it is and the answers we gave:

Q: How long will you be staying in Greece?
A: Quite a long time probably.
Q: What will the weather be like?
A: Hopefully much better than in England.
Q: Are you taking all your worldly possessions with you?

A: Yes, apart from quite a lot of books and several pairs of underpants which still had plenty of wear in them.

Q: When do you hope to return?

A: I just told you that in Question One.

Q: Will you be travelling alone?

A: Are you kidding?

Q: I'll ask the questions if you don't mind.

A: Sorry. The thing is, I'm feeling a bit stressed at the moment, what with all the burning bridges and upping sticks, not to mention the—

Q: Well?

A: Er… what was the question again?

Q: (sighing heavily) Will you be travelling alone?

A: No.

Q: What do you need to take with you?

A: So which part of "all our worldly possessions" did you not understand?

Q: Listen, sunshine, don't get stroppy with me. I'm only asking you these questions in an obviously futile attempt to stop you making a complete hashup of the whole business and ending up with all your savings haemorrhaging away like so many of the other halfwits I've come across.

A: Clean underwear.

Q: Pardon?

A: You asked me what we *needed* to take with us, and my mother always used to say that—

Q: Yes, yes, never mind that now. I want to get home to my tea. – What is your travel budget?

A: I'm not sure that's any of your business, but put down "limited" if you really want to know.

Q: Where is your destination?

A: Oh for— *Greece*. How many more times do I have to tell you? I mean, why on earth would we have bought your stupid book about moving to Greece if we were planning to move to Guatemala or the Turks and Caicos Islands? And quite frankly, I think this whole questionnaire is a complete— Wait a minute. Where are you going? – Come back here. You haven't asked me about the—

So that was the questionnaire double-checked, and a couple of days later we squeezed ourselves into the little space that remained in our rather elderly VW Transporter camper van and headed south. The van was so packed with "essentials" that you couldn't have swung a proverbial cat in it, although we didn't actually have a cat at the time, proverbial or otherwise. Instead, we had our Staffordshire Bull Terrier, Bessie, but she hated even being picked up, so the swinging experiment was never really a serious option.

Nor was it an option to take a leisurely meander down through Europe as we'd originally planned, and this too was because of Bessie. Not that it was her fault exactly. It was just the absurd amount of bureaucracy involved in the supposedly simple act of transporting a dog from one European country to another. When we'd first heard about the Pet Passport we'd need to get for her, we'd assumed it would be as straightforward as getting a human one, but that's probably why they say that "assume makes an ass of you and me". It took hour upon tedious hour of phone calls just to find out what we had to do and what paperwork we'd need to legally get Bessie from England to Greece, and in desperation, I ended up calling DEFRA (the Department for Environment, Food and Rural Affairs), which was responsible for implementing the Pet Passport Scheme.

'All I want to know is what I have to do to get a dog from England to Greece,' I said.

'No, it's not easy, is it?' said the man from the

ministry.

'Pardon?'

'The whole Pet Passport Scheme's a bit of a hotchpotch really.'

He was beginning to sound like Marvin the Paranoid Android.

'The thing is,' he went on, 'it was never really designed for domestic pets. It was just kind of... tagged on to the EU legislation for moving livestock, and to be perfectly honest, it would be a hell of a lot easier if you were transporting a herd of sheep or cattle.'

'Not in a camper van it wouldn't.'

'No, fair point.'

'Look,' I said, 'I don't mean to be disrespectful, but is there anyone else I can talk to about this? Your... superior or somebody.'

'Well, you could,' he said after a slow sucking in of breath, 'but the next person above me is the Minister of Agriculture himself, and I really don't think he'd have a clue what you were talking about.'

We did eventually get Bessie all the right jabs and official documents (or so we hoped) and she ended up with a file an inch thick all to herself. Part of the problem was that each EU country we were going to pass through had its own rules and regulations, even though the Pet Passport was intended to cover the whole of Europe. These included the maximum number of days you could have your pet dog/cat/gerbil/boa constrictor in each member state and varied widely. A particular anomaly was that we could have spent up to thirty days with Bessie in France but we were only allowed ten days to get her from the UK to Greece. Hence the need to forget about the leisurely meander and get a bit of a wriggle on – mainly because there was a strong likelihood that the van might break down and we'd have to use up several of our precious days while it languished in a French or Italian garage waiting for parts.

But as my mother often used to say to my brother and I when we were kids, "Never trouble trouble till trouble troubles you", which was rather ironic since she was the biggest worrier I've ever known. On this occasion, however, the advice would have been totally justified. The van behaved perfectly throughout the whole seventeen hundred miles from Calais, down through France and Italy to the port of Brindisi, where we caught the ferry to Igoumenitsa in northern Greece.

And not only was the trip itself almost entirely hassle free, never once did anyone show the slightest interest in checking Bessie's Pet Passport documents at any of the border controls. The race through Europe had therefore been completely unnecessary, and if we'd have been able to see into the future, we'd have taken a far more scenic route and visited some of the sights. In Italy, for instance, we spent one night on a campsite that was almost directly opposite the archaeological site of Pompeii, but we didn't get to look round it because it was closed by the time we arrived in the evening and we had to rush off again the following morning. This was a great pity as, by all accounts, it's an extraordinary place and even has some ancient – and incredibly raunchy – graffiti, which might have been interesting. As Robin Williams once said, 'Look at the walls of Pompeii. That's what got the Internet started.'

4

Snow Going Back

According to Wikipedia, it's a total myth that the Eskimos – or Inuit to give them their proper title – have lots and lots of words for "snow". The Sami (Laplanders) do, apparently. They have hundreds. But this is neither the time nor the place to get into a detailed analysis of the language of the "indigenous circumpolar people inhabiting a region which today encompasses parts of far northern Sweden, Norway, Finland, the Kola Peninsula of Russia, and the border area between south and middle Sweden and Norway". (Thank you, Wiki.)

No, the point I want to make here is that the Greeks don't have many words for snow because they don't come across it very often – not in southern Greece anyway. In fact, they only have one word for snow – *heeóni* – and translated literally, it means: "Where the bloody hell did all this white stuff come from?"

It therefore came as a bit of a shock when we first arrived in Greece in February 2004 to find that the whole place was knee deep in *heeóni*. The worst *heeóni* in thirty years. Athens Airport closed. Roads gridlocked. – One of the main reasons we'd come here was to escape the crap weather in Britain, and now here we were in the same bloody *heeóni* that had stopped the container lorry getting to our house in England when we moved out. But that was Derbyshire. The heart of the Peak District. A thousand foot above sea level in the middle of winter.

You expect it, for God's sake. Shedloads of it. But this was Greece – the land of sea, sand and perpetual sunshine where most people think Jack Frost is a subtitled TV detective show and ice is something you put in your ouzo.

Even the Greeks could talk about little else but the weather, which would of course have been perfectly normal in Britain where everyone is obsessed by it. It is by far the most frequent topic of conversation in the UK, and even complete strangers waiting for a bus will spend at least a couple of minutes discussing how good/bad the weather is at the moment and what it is likely to do later. It features heavily in almost every aspect of British life, and all forms of popular culture are riddled with it. For instance, whereas every other Greek song includes the words *s'agapó* ("I love you"), every other British song is about the weather – *Here Comes the Sun*, *It's Raining in My Heart* and *Fog on the Tyne* to name but a few. Many years ago, the ukelele-playing Lancastrian comedian George Formby even used the weather for his catchphrase, "Turned out nice again".

So endemic is this weather obsession in Britain that I believe it should be classified as a notifiable disease. As is the fashion these days, it could even be given its own TLA (three letter acronym) such as MOD – Meteorologically Obsessive Disorder. Don't be fooled into thinking that it's just a harmless way of passing a few minutes when you can't think of anything else to talk about. Oh no. The seriousness of the condition lies in its complete lack of foundation in logic, and sufferers should be pitied in much the same way as someone who goes around claiming to be Napoleon Bonaparte (unless of course he happens to be a short, balding Frenchman who was born in 1769 and was defeated at the Battle of Waterloo by the Duke of Wellington). My point is that, given that the weather in Britain is almost always rubbish, why do the Brits feel the need to talk about it all the time? Why not just accept that it's rubbish and talk about something more interesting like the price of fish? But no, we still have to have the incessantly repeated dialogues which go:

HE: Weather's a bit rubbish today.
SHE: Yes it is, isn't it.
HE: Do you think it'll be rubbish later on?
SHE: Probably.

I do have to confess that, as an Englishman myself, I am not in the least immune from the affliction of being weather obsessed – a true MOD sufferer in fact – and although we've lived in Greece for thirteen years now, I'm still a long way from being cured of my affliction. For instance, one day last summer when the temperature was almost forty degrees Celsius, I found myself saying 'Hot today, isn't it?' to the garage attendant who was filling our car with petrol. Not unnaturally, her response was to look at me quizzically, then up at the brilliantly blue sky, and then back at me again before shrugging and saying, 'It's August. What the hell did you expect?' Well, she had a point of course, but I don't like silences and I had to say *something*. Perhaps she'd have engaged more if I'd said, 'I see the price of red mullet's gone up again.'

But back to our snowy arrival in Greece…

Penny has always had a reputation for being a bit of a jinx on the weather, and before we left England, several people jokingly said they'd probably pick up a paper one day and read the massive banner headline: "GREEK TOURISM INDUSTRY COLLAPSES – ENGLISH WOMAN RESPONSIBLE FOR WORST WEATHER SINCE RECORDS BEGAN". Fairly amusing at the time but a lot less funny when we found ourselves slithering around on the ridiculously icy mountain roads of southern Greece, at night, in our rear-wheel-drive VW camper van, trying to remember who the Greek god of slithering camper vans was so we could get some serious praying in. It was a bit like being trapped inside an out of control curling stone without having someone in front of you with a brush. (Curling, incidentally, is a sport which I once heard described as "housework on ice". Billy Connolly, I think.) And as for gritting lorries, forget it. There isn't even a translation for "gritting lorry" in my Greek dictionary, and it's a pretty big dictionary, believe me.

We did eventually make it in one piece to the house we were renting near Stoupa – the same area where we'd had a holiday the previous year – although I use the word "renting" loosely. By an amazing stroke of good fortune (for a change), it was owned by a friend of Penny's in England, and she was delighted to have someone living there over the winter when it would otherwise have been empty. So delighted was she that she didn't even charge us any rent, and all we had to pay were the utility bills.

It was a really nice house with great views and very tastefully designed. One of the things that struck me as a little odd about it, though, was that it was upside down. I don't mean that the roof was where the basement should have been or you had to have sticky Spiderman pads on your feet to get around, just that the bedrooms and bathroom were downstairs and the living room and kitchen upstairs. This meant that the main bedroom was almost half underground and had one very long window that was only about a foot high, so when I woke up on the first morning I thought I'd been posted and was trapped inside some kind of huge pillar box. Quite scary at the time, but I got used to it after a while and no longer felt the need to stick a "FRAGILE – THIS WAY UP" label on my forehead before going to bed every night.

Another issue about the rented house was that it didn't have a landline telephone, and it was a major problem being without Internet access, especially as it meant I couldn't check on essential items of world news such as the latest football scores. (Crystal Palace were doing uncharacteristically well that season, as I recall.) Not to be thwarted, however, we found out that the next door house, which was unoccupied at the time, *did* have a landline so we could plug into that – with the owners' permission of course. All we had to do was pick up a cheap phone – easy – and about thirty metres of extension cable. Not so easy.

OTE – Greece's version of British Telecom but, amazing as this may seem, even less efficient – has a big shop in Kalamata, which is the major city for the area, so that's where we headed for our pre-packed plug-and-play extension cable. Except they don't exist. Not like that anyway. They could sell us the cable, but we'd have to go somewhere else altogether to get a plug fitted on each end.

'Well, all right,' I said. 'So can we have some cable then, please?'

'Sure,' said the OTE guy. 'How many kilos you want?'

'You're kidding me, right?'

There was a brief deadpan pause and then a hearty got-you-there-mate laugh. 'Yeah, of course I'm kidding. This is telephone cable we're talking about – not rope or string.'

'O...kay, I'll have thirty metres then.'

'Is it for indoors or outdoors?'

'Er, both really.'

'Sorry, but we've had a bit of a run on indoor/outdoor cable lately, and we've only got ten metres left. Will that be enough?'

'Not unless it's very stretchy, no.'

The OTE guy then helpfully gave us directions to a shop which he was certain would have more cable than you'd need to set up a direct line all the way back to the UK, so off we went. We got the cable but still had to go to a different shop to get the plugs fitted of course.

This was probably one of our earliest first-hand experiences of the old adage that we came to know and dread – "In Greece, nothing is impossible, but everything is difficult" (*stın Elláda, típota den eínaı adýnato, allá ta pánta eínaı dýskola*). But more of that later. The important thing was that we were finally here in Greece, having ticked stick upping and bridge burning off our list of "101 Metaphors We Plan to Achieve During Our Lifetime", and now we'd come to a different bridge altogether. This was the one we had to cross when we came to it because, well, we'd come to it, and the name of this particular bridge was "Finding Our Dream Home" as several of the moving abroad books so nauseatingly put it. Another day, another metaphor, except this one took rather more than a day to cross off the list.

5

A Pleasant and Enjoyable Experience?

It goes without saying (but I'm going to say it anyway) that moving to a foreign country can be a daunting prospect for even the most intrepid of people, and not being particularly intrepid ourselves, Penny and I had been determined that we'd be as well prepared as we could be for such a life-changing event. This included reading just about everything that had ever been written on the subject of moving abroad and particularly if it was about Greece of course. Once we were here, however, we soon realised how much of this stuff was inaccurate, out of date or just plain wrong. Here's a quote from the blurb on the back of one of the books, *Buying a Home in Greece and Cyprus* by Joanna Styles (2001): This book "is designed to guide you through the jungle and make it"... i.e. buying a property in Greece... "a pleasant and enjoyable experience".

A pleasant and enjoyable experience? Buying any house is never going to be pleasant and enjoyable even in your own country where you're fluent in the language and have at least a reasonable knowledge of the process involved. Buying and selling a house is supposed to be the second most stressful life event after bereavement, isn't it? I find choosing between different brands of frozen peas in the supermarket brings me to the verge of a nervous breakdown, and that's in the UK where I can understand what it says on the labels.

But pleasant and enjoyable or not, we had at least decided on a specific area we wanted to focus on, which was near a small town called Kyparissia on the west coast of the Peloponnese. The reason for this somewhat uncharacteristic decisiveness (on my part anyway) was that Penny had spotted a five-acre smallholding on an estate agent's website long before we came out here, and the views alone looked – and I hesitate to use the word – awesome. There was a small house at the top of the land, which was set in a natural amphitheatre of mountains and rolling hills, and from its height of about three hundred metres above sea level, the panorama of a perfectly curved bay with typically Greek blue waters was straight out of a picture postcard.

So, "Xerika", as it's called, was the first place we went to visit, having first checked to see if it was still for sale. Amazingly after all that time, it was, although there were plenty of reasons why nobody else had been mad enough to snap it up in the meantime, but more on that later.

Even after we'd been to see the place and realised it was every bit as "awesome" as we'd been led to believe, we thought we should at least have a look around to see what else was available before we rushed into a decision we might later regret. So that's what we did – traipsed round a whole load of other properties that were on the market and then meandered carefully into a decision we might later regret.

There was one estate agent – a Brit who will remain anonymous because I wouldn't want him to benefit from the old adage that all publicity is good publicity – and he showed us a few places, one of which we really liked. It was much further inland than Xerika, but it was almost as remote and had a similar amount of land with a small house that was in fairly good condition. Once he'd given us the guided tour, the agent let us have a good poke round on our own, but that's when we came to the damning realisation that the surrounding hills and mountains, although strikingly impressive, meant you'd never get a proper sunset.

'So what do you think?' said the agent when we'd finished our mooching.

'Um... it's great except...'

'Except?'

'Er, no sunset. You'd never get one.'

'Pah,' said the agent with the soul of a comatose Vulcan. 'Seen one sunset, seen 'em all if you ask me.'

Well, we hadn't asked him, and we didn't find his painstakingly reasoned argument in the least convincing, so we buggered off and left him to it.

The other places we looked at that were of any interest – and did have sunsets – were also in fairly remote areas, so there were no street names or numbers. Not even quaint villagey house names like "Rose Cottage" or "Silage View". Consequently, we had to give them nicknames so we'd remember which one we were talking about when we were drawing up the inevitable pros and cons lists. There was "The Pink House", for instance, one of the cons of which was the eponymous colour, but that came under the column headed "Easily Remedied". Much less easy would be how to tilt the entire house back to a position where the spirit level bubble didn't disappear altogether. It gave new meaning to the phrase "run down" because as soon as you entered, the sloping wooden floor meant you couldn't help but run down it at such a speed that you were in serious danger of crashing headlong through the window at the far end of the room. The window was in fact already broken, so perhaps this had been the fate of some other prospective purchaser who'd been a little less cautious than we were.

Then there was "The Avocado House", so nicknamed because the main feature that appealed to us was the pair of very mature avocado trees which were so overladen with fruit, you could have filled two large carrier bags just with the avocados that were strewn around on the ground. The asking price would have been well worth it for the avocados alone. The rest of the land was stuffed with veg plots and other assorted fruit trees, and the house itself was – as the estate agents would put it – very well maintained. The downside? No views. And this, like the aforementioned lack of sunsets, was a major deal breaker according to our pros and cons list. I must admit, though, that I still get the odd twinge of regret whenever I see the price of avocados in the shops.

Incidentally, whenever we do go mad and lash out on the occasional avocado, Penny insists on having her half with lemon and sugar rather than the more traditional – and, dare I say, socially acceptable – vinaigrette or mayonnaise. Lemon and sugar? That's about as weird as pouring gravy on your cornflakes or eating Marmite for breakfast. As the old saying goes, "There's nowt so queer as folk, 'cept thee and me, and I'm not so sure about thee".

Anyway, back to the plot. Or perhaps I should say back to looking at properties *without* much of a plot. The thing was, having looked round a whole load of places that were about the size of a substantial smallholding, we began to ask ourselves the question, "Do we really want a place with a lot of land?" So we told the local estate agent we'd been dealing with – not the comatose Vulcan one, a different one – that we wanted to see whatever properties they'd got which just had a good-sized garden.

'But you said you wanted somewhere with about five acres,' said the very nice German woman in a tone which suggested she might have started the sentence with a "*donner und blitzen*" and a slap of the palm to the forehead. (For the sake of accuracy and due deference to the metric system, I should point out that she didn't actually say "five acres" but "twenty thousand square metres", otherwise known as twenty *strémmata* to use the Greek term.)

Despite her understandable indignation, she did show us round some houses that had considerably less land than we'd originally asked for, and one of them – "The Blue-Shuttered House" as we called it – took my fancy big time. It was in really good nick, but most appealingly, it came fully furnished with beds and chairs, pots and pans, cups and saucers and everything else you could wish for, right down to some rather elegant-looking placemats and coasters. There was even a windsurfer, complete with its own zip-up protective cover.

The whole place was like a much tidier and more up-market version of the *Marie Celeste*. The rather sad reason for this, though, as the agent told us, was that it belonged to a young German couple who'd bought it when they'd moved to Greece soon after they'd got married. Within just a few short weeks, however, they both realised they'd made a big mistake – about each other and not the house, apparently – and gone their separate ways, vanishing into the night with only a few of their most prized possessions.

It was a sad story of course, and call me heartless if you like, but I wasn't going to let that come between me and all those free gifts. It was perfect. No decorating. No DIY. No trudging round kitchenware shops checking out the latest bargains in stainless steel cooking utensils. All we had to do was move in and start living. Kick off our shoes, sit back and have a leisurely trawl through YouTube for some idiotproof tutorials on windsurfing for beginners.

Penny, on the other hand, had different ideas.

'The trouble is,' she said after I'd already filled up two and a half pages of the pros column later that evening, 'it's a bit *too* perfect.'

'What do you mean "too perfect"? How can it be too perfect?'

'Well, we wouldn't need to do anything to it.'

'Exactly.'

'So we wouldn't be able to make it... our own.'

'Yes we would. That's what it means when you buy a house. We hand over the asking price and it's ours. How much more "our own" do you want?'

There was an ominous pause, accompanied by one of those looks which told me in no uncertain terms that: "Not only do you have no discernible soul, but it is patently obvious that all you're interested in is getting out of doing any decorating or DIY".

'That's not true,' I said, thinking that she'd spoken this aloud and trying to muster a similar level of indignation we'd witnessed from our estate agent earlier in the day.

'What's not true?'

'Oh, sorry, I thought you said something.'

But the battle was lost. Well, hardly a battle really. More like the kind of humiliating trouncing someone like Accrington Stanley would suffer if they managed to get to the later rounds of the FA Cup and drew Man United at Old Trafford. The only difference being that Accrington Stanley would at least benefit financially from the mauling.

'It's got a free windsurfer,' I added lamely in a last ditch but ultimately futile attempt to force the game into extra time. 'It's even got its own zip-up protective cover!'

'The house?'

'The windsurfer.'

But it was a poor strike from long range which barely made it to the edge of the penalty area, and needless to say, I left the field of play with head hung low after suffering the house-hunting equivalent of a twenty-seven nil annihilation.

They think it's all over? Ken, it was over before it started.

So – rather foolishly in my opinion – we didn't snap up "The Blue-Shuttered House" despite its wallet-watering abundance of free gifts. Penny, by the way, tried to argue that they weren't free at all and the vendors had probably added on a wodge to the sale price to cover them. Some people just don't get the whole concept of free gifts, do they?

6

And the Winner Is...

It came to the point during the quest for our "dream home" where neither of us could bear the thought of traipsing round yet another Pink House, Avocado House, Blue-Shuttered House or any other "desirable properties" the estate agents decided to throw at us. More importantly, the stress involved in the whole house-hunting business was starting to get to both of us and resulted in several – sometimes completely irrational – arguments.

One such recurring argument was – and I hesitate to say this – mostly my fault and was usually along the following lines:

ME: Well, I never wanted to move to Greece in the first place.

PENNY: So you keep saying.

ME: Spain. That's where I wanted to go. I mean, it made perfect financial sense for a start. We already had the *Rough Guide to Spain*, a Spanish road atlas *and* the Spanish Linguaphone course. What did we have for Greece?

PENNY: Nothing until you bought me the *Rough Guide to Greece* and the BBC Greek language course for my birthday.

ME: Yes, but that was only after you'd said

you'd rather move to Cleethorpes than Spain because you'd once been to Torremolinos or wherever on holiday and a waiter was rude to you.

Penny has always insisted that this wasn't the reason why she didn't want to move to Spain, but either way, it was arguments such as these which finally convinced us that it was time to gather together the reams of pros and cons lists and make a decision.

This was when we came to the not at all surprising realisation that the clear winner of "Finding a Place to Live in Greece 2004" was Xerika – the very place we'd seen on the Internet even before we'd left England and well before we'd wasted vast amounts of time, energy, arguments and paper for pros and cons lists in our search for somewhere that might be... "just that little bit better".

Not that we hadn't had a few niggling doubts about Xerika when we'd first spotted it on the estate agent's website, despite the photos of the stunning views and the typically gushing blurb: "The estate dominates the region from a slope high above this picturesque village on the side of the mountains which surround Kyparissia". Estate? Dominates? High above? What was it? Some kind of medieval castle? But then came the words which gave us our first niggling doubt: "The single storey house is functionally designed". Uh-oh. I was beginning to sense the medieval dungeon part of the castle without the castle itself.

Our second niggling doubt arose from the website's description of the "well established vegetation". Hmm. What now? A medieval dungeon surrounded by a jungle so dense you'd need a machete and chainsaw just to get to the place? Not to mention living in mortal fear of bumping into David Attenborough and a BBC film crew every time you ventured out of the house.

In reality, the description of the house as "functionally designed" simply meant that it was very small. A bijou-sized fifty-five square metres, consisting of one bedroom, a minute bathroom, a combined living room/kitchen and a couple of small sheds. But so what? We'd be living outdoors for most of the time. Wasn't that one of the main reasons we'd moved to Greece in the first place? And in this case, outdoors meant two large terraces and five acres of land.

As for the "well established vegetation", we were relieved to see on our first visit that this was mostly grass – very long grass, it has to be said, but nothing a good scything with a quality, top-of-the-range Stihl strimmer couldn't handle. (People at Stihl-dot-com – manufacturers and purveyors of agricultural and horticultural machinery – please note blatant product placement there.)

In addition to the grass, the well established vegetation may even have been intended to include the four hundred and twenty mature olive trees, sixty assorted fruit and nut trees and seventy grapevines. But whatever the intention, that's exactly what we'd be getting, and this leads me to another niggling doubt I had when we first went to see the place.

'Four hundred and twenty olive trees,' said the agent, beaming with what – for an estate agent – seemed to be perfectly genuine enthusiasm. 'Best olive oil in the world.'

'But we don't know the first thing about growing olives,' I said, wondering if the cultivation methods were anything like those for growing extremely large broccoli plants.

'It's not exactly rocket science,' said the agent – or words to that effect. 'You'll soon pick it up.'

In hindsight, and with thirteen years' experience as an olive farmer, I have to grudgingly admit that she was telling the truth. There really isn't anything complicated about growing olives. However – and this is a big "however" – it does involve periods of sheer bloody hard work and mind-numbing tedium. As for the olive harvest itself, this is an activity which should be registered with the Dangerous Sports Association and causes me night sweats for several months in advance. But that's a story for later on.

Niggling doubts aside, we'd made the decision that Xerika was the place for us, and all we had to do now was buy it. As we should have predicted, though, the conveyancing process didn't go as smoothly as we'd have hoped, and before you start bracing yourself for an extended rant about Greek bureaucracy, I have to tell you that it was the *Brits* who very nearly screwed up the whole transaction. To be precise, the [*Bleep*] Building Society. And if you're wondering whether that bleep is in place of an expletive or the name of the building society in question, you can take your pick. The two are pretty much synonymous.

Once we'd agreed the sale price with Xerika's owner, the next job was to get our building society in the UK to transfer the money to our Greek bank account. It really shouldn't have been too difficult an operation, but the [*Bleep*] Building Society apparently decided otherwise. Having printed out their ridiculously long and detailed form from the Internet, carefully filled it in and posted it to them, we waited for the transfer to be carried out... and waited... and waited... and waited. After frequent visits to our Greek bank and finding that the money still hadn't arrived, we contacted the building society to discover that the reason it hadn't arrived was because they hadn't actually sent it. Their explanation was that: 'The amount you requested would have overdrawn your account.'

'No it wouldn't.'

'Yes it would.'

'No it wouldn't.'

'Yes it would.'

Now, I enjoy a good bit of pantomime banter as much as the next person – which is probably not a lot – but this was just getting silly, so I told Widow Twankey I wanted to talk to someone higher up the cast list. Preferably Aladdin himself – or herself to be strictly politically correct and also in deference to the time-honoured transgender traditions of the great British pantomime.

This seemed to do the trick, and eventually Aladdin (it was in fact a "him") realised that one of his minions (quite possibly the wicked Abanazar) had misread our form and thought we'd requested the money in pounds (which would indeed have overdrawn our account) rather than euros (which wouldn't have overdrawn our account, and which we'd quite clearly stated in six different places on their own bloody form in the first place).

Still, it was just a simple clerical error that could be easily rectified... couldn't it?

Apparently not.

'I'm afraid the form which you originally submitted has been destroyed,' said Aladdin.

'Oh,' I said. 'What happened? Was there a fire or something?'

'It's company policy.'

'What, to start fires?'

'To prevent money laundering.'

I laughed, of course, but I could tell by the stony silence at the other end of the line that he wasn't joking.

'So what do we do now?' I said.

'If you pop into your local branch, they'll give you a new form to fill in.'

I pointed out that since we were in Greece and that, to my certain knowledge, the nearest branch of the [*Bleep*]

Building Society was about a thousand miles away, "popping in" was hardly an option. Aladdin then suggested some nonsense about transferring the money into a friend's account so they could forward it on to us. Oddly enough, he didn't seem to think this would look like money laundering at all, but after further discussion a compromise was eventually reached. This involved printing out another form from the Internet, filling it in and then – because we didn't have access to a scanner and speed was now of the essence – faxing it to the building society.

This time, the money did finally arrive in our Greek bank account, and the whole deal for buying Xerika was signed and sealed and – this being Greece – stamped about a dozen times. Greek officials just love their rubber stamps, and in this case it was one of the town's public notaries, whose job it is to see that everything about a property sale is legal and above board. Also – and this is Number 27 on my list of "Rather Bizarre Things About Greece" – the notary has to approve what's called the "notional value" of the property. This means that you agree an amount that is quite a lot less than what you actually paid for it, and that's the sum you pay tax on. It's not some sort of fiddle either. It's an officially recognised part of the whole conveyancing rigmarole, and is of course good news for the buyer, of no interest whatsoever to the seller, but makes absolutely no economic sense at all in terms of swelling the state's coffers with much needed euros. This is perhaps one of many reasons why Greece has found itself in such deep financial poo and why the likes of Angela Merkel and the International Monetary Fund insisted that all future Greek finance ministers would have to read – and be tested on – *Economics for Dummies* before taking office. (Naturally, this wouldn't have applied to Yanis Varoufakis, who was all too briefly Greece's finance minister in 2015 and has taught economics at various universities around the world, including Cambridge.)

7

A Fridge Too Far

Most of the "Buying Your Dream Home in Greece" type of books often include opinions on the "desirability" or otherwise of various different regions, and this is what one of the authors (Joanna Styles) had to say about the area of the Peloponnese where Xerika is:

"On the west coast are some of the best beaches in Greece, although their remoteness and the general lack of development in the area make them rather inaccessible."

Rather inaccessible? Oh really? Well, we managed to get here all right in our beat-up old camper van, and judging by the other vehicles on the road, so did quite a few other people. We found that the use of dog sleds, high altitude breathing equipment and other similar paraphernalia were entirely superfluous to our own particular expedition to the lost world of the western Peloponnese. There's even an airport within perfectly easy range for your average camel train.

Maybe the book was written before the invention of the internal combustion engine or even tarmac. But no. I checked. First published in 2000 with a second edition in 2001. If you want inaccessible, try Aberystwyth. And before I get cartloads of hate mail from any born-and-bred Aberystwythians who might be reading this, I happened to live there for three years, so I know what I'm talking about.

The western Peloponnese isn't inaccessible by any stretch of the imagination, although the onward journey from sea level to Xerika itself was – and still is – a complete nightmare. As one of our early visitors remarked, 'Well, at least you won't be bothered by Jehovah's Witnesses up here.' Five uphill kilometres of potholes the size of small meteor craters, loose stones and dirt which turns to a river of mud after a few millimetres of rain is not the kind of carefree motoring environment the VW camper van was designed for.

The whole area is riddled with these kinds of tracks, mostly to provide access to the many hundreds of olive groves, and before the beginning of the economic crisis in Greece, the local authority used to repair most of them about once a year. This was usually a little in advance of the olive harvesting season, and the repair work generally consisted of sending up a JCB to smooth over the worst of the craters and fill the rest of the potholes with sand. Not surprisingly, most of this got washed away as soon as we had the first downpour of rain, but we were still glad to have a few days – sometimes weeks – when we could drive up and down our track in relatively jolt-free comfort.

Nowadays, though, the local authority doesn't have the funds to pay for even these temporary repairs – except, that is, if there's an election looming. For some reason, whichever political party happens to be in power at the time seems to think that fixing these dirt tracks is a real vote winner despite their almost total neglect since the previous election. This means that during the four years between elections, the only reason our track is passable in anything less than a Sherman tank is because of Penny and I and our shovels and spades. Truth be told, however, there's not a lot of whistling while we work.

For our first eighteen months at Xerika, and before we

were finally forced to accept that a vehicle with four wheel drive was something of a necessity, our only means of transport was the camper van. This was difficult enough during the winter rains, but even going downhill in the summer when the track was at least dry was – excuse the expression – hell on wheels. Without the benefit of air conditioning or being able to go above three miles an hour to get any kind of breeze through the open windows, we were wringing with sweat by the time we reached the main road. A change of clothes was therefore essential before we could venture into town and submit ourselves to the olfactory scrutiny of polite society.

Many a low slung vehicle has parted company with its sump on its way up to our place, and this is why – in our pre four-by-four days – we chickened out of bringing the van up the last particularly horrendous stretch of track below the house. Instead, we parked it in a small clearing and trudged the last kilometre or so, lugging whatever we'd happened to hunter-gather in town, regardless of sweltering heat or torrential rain. This could have presented us with a serious problem when we first moved in to a fridgeless and cookerless Xerika and realised we'd have to rectify this situation pretty damn quick if we didn't want to starve to death.

As it turned out, though, getting the fridge up to the house wasn't an issue. Nikos, the guy in the shop where we bought it, just came straight out with the music-to-my-ears question: 'When do you want it delivered?'

'As soon as possible?' I said it more like a question than a statement, expecting the usual Comet-stroke-Dixons-stroke-Argos-type response of a shrug and a sigh and a: 'Hmm. Looks like we won't have a van in your area till a week next Friday.'

But instead, Nikos floored me with a: 'Would now be okay?'

'What, as in... now?' I had to grab the edge of the counter to stop myself from falling. He didn't even try and sell me some useless extended warranty like they always do in the UK. What was more, there wouldn't be any extra charge for delivery.

As we've discovered since then, getting stuff delivered comes under the heading of "Things Which Are Better in Greece Than They Are in Britain". Whether it's fridges, timber or bags of cement, there's never any of the week-next-Friday nonsense. There was even one time when the builders' merchant's truck got here before we did.

Having sorted out the problem of getting the fridge up to the house, we still had the issue of the two-ring cooker hob we'd just bought in a different shop and, more importantly, the ten kilo gas bottle that went with it. I decided to try it on, knowing full well that if I'd dared to suggest such a thing in Britain, I'd get a response involving several sharp intakes of breath, a lot of tutting and a five-minute lecture about company policy on health and safety.

Not with Nikos I didn't. 'Of course,' he said. 'I'll bring it up with the fridge.'

And so it was that Penny went in the pickup with Nikos and his mate to show them the way, and I followed on in the van with Penny's seventy-odd year old mum, who was staying with us at the time. She and I had left the van in its usual parking space and had just set off up the hill with half a dozen carrier bags of groceries when we met Nikos coming back down the track in his now empty pickup.

He pulled over. 'What are you doing with all those bags?'

'Er, taking them up to the house?'

'But I could have taken all those in the pickup too,' he said, giving himself a full-blooded slap of the palm to his forehead. 'I am such an idiot. I should have asked if you had anything else to bring up.'

It was all I could do to persuade him that it really wasn't his fault and that it was totally unnecessary for him to drive a couple of kilometres further down the track to find a spot where he could turn round and then ferry us and our bags up to the house.

I said earlier that nothing is impossible in Greece, but everything is difficult. Nikos clearly demonstrated that this isn't always the case and that some things are much easier than you could possibly have hoped. The same, however, could not be said of our first night at Xerika.

8

Belching Bertha

Strictly speaking, "Xerika" is the name of our immediate area rather than the house itself, but we thought it sounded better than something naff like "Homer Sweet Homer", "Acropolis Cottage" or "Dun-oliveharvesting". In Ancient Greek, the word *xerıká* means "dry land". In modern Greek, *xerós* means "dry", from which we get the English word "xeric", meaning "of, relating to, or growing in dry conditions". Apparently, there's even such a thing as "xeriscaping", which is all about gardening without much water.

There was nothing dry about our first night at Xerika, however. Not that it rained. It didn't. It was the end of May and already getting hot, which was why we were a bit reluctant to light the big open fire in the living room to run the back boiler. But how else were we going to have hot water for our morning ablutions? There was no mains electricity, and it would have taken forever to heat up enough water on the new gas hob, given the limited number and size of pans we had. As for the oil-fired boiler for the central heating system, it looked like it had last been used about the time of the Siege of Troy, so we weren't going to risk it until it had been properly checked out. The only option was the back boiler behind the fireplace, which the estate agent had assured us was in perfect working order.

Since it was already stifling inside the house, we

decided that we'd light a small fire just before going to bed, which would hopefully keep going through the night and give us plenty of piping hot water the next day. "Going to bed" was somewhat of an exaggeration, though, as the container full of most of our worldly belongings was still in Athens, and all we had with us were a couple of double airbeds. Penny's mum had one in the bedroom, and Penny and I had the other in the living room – as far away from the fire as possible.

When I woke up in the middle of the night feeling uncomfortably damp, my first thought was that I was simply sweating profusely as a result of sleeping inside an oven the size of a small house. But then I became conscious of the fact that my left hand – which was hanging over the side of the airbed – seemed to be considerably wetter than the rest of me.

Curious to unravel the mystery of this strange anatomical phenomenon of why my left hand should be sweating a lot more than any other part of my body, I switched on the bedside torch to find that the entire floor was awash with a rust-coloured liquid which may once have resembled water. On further investigation, I discovered that the liquid was also quite warm, thus demonstrating that the back boiler had done its job after all. Unfortunately, however, it had decided to release its contents several hours earlier than required, and although the entire subject of physics has always remained a closed book to me – mainly because I never felt the need or desire to open the book in the first place – it wouldn't have taken a Stephen Hawking to figure out what had gone wrong. The heating of the water had presumably increased the pressure inside the boiler to the extent that it had become more than a match for a weak spot – or more likely, several weak spots – in the metal.

Not being one to create a drama out of a crisis and with the utmost consideration for the still sleeping

Penny, I took it upon myself to tackle the flood single-handedly and as quietly as possible. The fire had already gone out by now, so all that remained was the mopping up operation. Everything was going – and I hesitate to use the word – swimmingly until the mop suddenly became unclipped from the clip inside the bucket where I had temporarily clipped it, and the handle came crashing down on the side of Penny's slumbering head. To this day, she still claims that it was a deliberate act on my part to "accidentally" wake her up by dropping a mop handle on her head so she'd then feel obliged to help with the xerification of the living room floor. (If "xerification" isn't a real word already, it is now.)

As if "The Annoying Incident of the Back Boiler in the Night-time" wasn't enough to start my karma haemorrhaging away, daylight was to bring its own share of trials and tribulations. I mentioned above that there was no mains electricity when we first moved in to Xerika (and nor was there for a further eighteen months), but what we did have was Belching Bertha. This was a massive and very ancient generator which was kept in a small shed about fifty yards or so from the house and was to become my arch nemesis over the next few weeks and months. We hadn't bothered firing it up on the first night, but we needed to get our shiny new fridge up and running, so I couldn't put it off any longer.

Apart from the fact that the generator shed was almost ankle deep in grease and oil, the filler cap for the fuel tank was less than a foot below an asbestos roof, and it was almost impossible to avoid scraping the asbestos with the back of my hand or the funnel every time I topped up with diesel. Because of the angle and my vain attempt to avoid whacking the asbestos, about half the diesel would end up in the tank, and the rest would invariably dribble all the way down the length of my arm. But once I'd eventually got a reasonable amount of diesel into the tank, all that remained was to start the engine, although this was no mean feat in itself.

A slight design fault in the system meant that the ignition was on the far side of the shed and furthest away from the doorway, so when the generator did actually start – usually on about the twenty-seventh time of asking but sometimes not at all – the first thing to happen was I got a facefull of thick black smoke from the exhaust before I could get out of the shed. (Hence the name, Belching Bertha.) But that wasn't the end of the operation. The volt meter was inside the house, and Penny had to shout to me to increase or decrease the revs until the required voltage was achieved, which often took several minutes as I struggled to hear her over the din of the generator.

Firing up Belching Bertha was a daily task for about a year and a half until we could get our mains electricity connected, and we probably wouldn't have bothered with it at all if we hadn't had to give the fridge a regular boost. We'd only run the generator for three hours or so from about seven in the evening, but it was something I began to dread from about four o'clock every afternoon. This was particularly true in the height of the summer when the belching black smoke and the stink of diesel combined with the asbestos-lined heat in the shed to produce an atmosphere which would have made the Black Hole of Calcutta seem like the honeymoon suite at the Ritz.

But since this chapter seems to be turning into little more than an extended moan, perhaps I should redress the balance with something rather more positive. By the time we moved in to Xerika at the end of May, the weather was perfect, and I decided that a gloating email to the "folks back home" was well overdue:

> *Dear All-of-you-shivering-in-the-cold-back-in-dear-old-Blighty,*

As it's too hot to do much outdoors, I thought I'd come in and write to you about our early impressions of living in Greece...

Some good things we've noticed about Greece so far:

1. *People seem to want to give you things for free. (Supermarkets often have signs saying: "Get one free, and while you're at it you may as well have a couple more for nothing to save you the trouble of coming back again". At least, we think that's what the signs translate as.)*
2. *You can get petrol for about fifty pence a litre and rather good wine for about seventy pence a litre.*
3. *Public transport is not only ridiculously cheap, but unlike in the UK, is almost always on time.*
4. *Wherever you are reading this, the weather is much better in Greece than where you are unless you happen to be somewhere like Barbados, which I very much doubt.*
5. *Garage labour charges seem to be less than £10 an hour.*
6. *Shops will giftwrap stuff for no extra charge, which makes even the crappiest present look expensive (at least until it's been opened).*

Some bad things we've noticed about Greece so far:

1. *A tin of Heinz Baked Beans costs about as much as a tin of Beluga caviar.*
2. *You can't get mature cheddar cheese anywhere.*

3. *They have snakes, scorpions and all sorts of other wildlife that seem intent on stinging, biting and/or strangling you to death at the slightest opportunity.*

4. *If you order a coffee, it comes in something the size of an eggcup with nineteen heaped teaspoons of Extra Strength Gold Blend and hardly any water, so you have to chew it rather than drink it. (In some places, you can order your coffee "pre-chewed", but we haven't tried this as we suspect that the proprietors might be exploiting migrant workers.)*

5. *The alphabet is very odd.*

Some things we've noticed about Greece but aren't yet sure if they're good or bad:

1. *Elderly people flag you down and demand to be given lifts – sometimes to different countries.*

2. *Kitchen work-surfaces here are several inches lower than in the UK. This means that anyone over five-foot-three gets a backache doing the washing-up. Apparently, this is because Greek men never cook or wash up. (Penny says this should go in the "Bad Things About Greece" section.)*

So, as you can see, the reasons for living in Greece far outweigh the reasons for not living in Greece. Okay, so it's only by one point so far, but it's early days yet. Statistically, therefore, living in Greece is a "good thing".

In the thirteen years since I wrote this email, quite a few of these things have changed, largely due to the rocketing prices of most of the items that were very cheap when we first came to Greece. Other things haven't changed at all. For instance, snakes, scorpions and other bitey/stingy creatures are as plentiful as ever, and the alphabet is still odd. But even though there's been a shift in my original statistical analysis, living in Greece still seems to be "a good thing".

9

You Don't Wanna Do It Like That

Because Xerika is so remote and the tracks to get here are in such a dreadful state, there's very little passing traffic except during the olive harvesting season when it's bordering on bedlam. During our first few days here, however, we had a steady stream of local farmers dropping by to welcome us and wish us *kalorízıko*, which means "good root" but effectively translates as "good luck". It's a word that's generally used in a situation like this when someone has moved into a new house, but it can also be used on almost every occasion when somebody has acquired anything new – a new car, a new fishing rod, and even a new hairdo, although in the last example "good roots" might have a more literal meaning and be intended as a compliment.

Reassuringly heart-warming as it was that so many people took the time and trouble to come and wish us well, we also suspected that there was an ulterior motive. Most Greeks are incredibly inquisitive, so this was a perfect opportunity to give not only ourselves a thorough looking over but also our various goods and chattels. They also tend to be unashamedly direct in the questions they ask, such as "How much did you pay for that car/fridge/breadknife/saucepan?", and however much you tell them it cost, the response is almost invariably a heavy frown and a "*Poh, poh, poh!*", which essentially means "Blimey, they saw you coming, didn't they?"

Since our early encounters with this sort of reaction, I've made it a policy to halve the real cost of anything I'm asked about, but I still get exactly the same frown and its accompanying "*Poh, poh, poh!*". I'm convinced that it wouldn't be any different even if I bought a brand new Rolls-Royce and said it cost me fifty euros. Sadly, though, a lack of the financial wherewithal means that this will have to remain an unproven theory for the time being at least.

Every so often, we've even been asked how much money we earn, and since Penny and I had both been brought up as reserved Brits who wouldn't dream of asking such questions, we were rather taken aback by this kind of direct monetary interrogation. But like so many of the other cultural differences, we've gradually got used to it, and nowadays we sometimes even resort to it ourselves.

Another thing we noticed about the Greek character very early on is that they love to give advice whether you've asked for it or not. Over the years, we've frequently been subjected to a whole range of suggestions and recommendations about whatever it is we happen to be doing at the time – or should have done but hadn't. This was certainly true of Pavlos, who was one of our earliest visitors and had come to tow away a knackered tractor from our land. No sooner had he wished us *kaloríziko* and had a good poke round the few belongings we'd brought with us from England than he marched over to one of the olive trees and told us that it was in desperate need of pruning. And not just that one either. Apparently, all four hundred and twenty of them needed doing.

'What, now?' I said.

'They should have been done weeks ago,' said Pavlos.

Given that the estate agent had assured us that we wouldn't need to do anything at all with the olive trees until the harvest in November, this came as somewhat of a shock, especially as we had no more idea of how to prune an olive tree than solve the international debt crisis. But Pavlos was more than happy to demonstrate the ancient and noble art, and magically producing a pruning saw from somewhere about his person, he set about the nearest tree. So quickly did he work, it was like a scene straight out of *Edward Scissorhands*, but ten minutes and a couple of trees later, we were pretty sure we'd got the hang of it, and Pavlos left us to it.

After about three hours, we'd successfully pruned one and a half trees, and it was at this point that father and son farmer duo, Thanassis and Yiorgos, called in to introduce themselves. But the moment the exchange of names and the *kalorízıko*'s were out of the way, Yiorgos – the son – pointed to the tree we were currently working on, and the following conversation ensued. Well, I say "conversation", but since our Greek was still extremely basic at the time and Yiorgos and Thanassis spoke no English whatsoever – and also spoke very quickly and at the same time – it was more like a mime show with mutually incomprehensible babbling. But this was the gist of it:

'What are you doing?' says Yiorgos.

'Er, pruning the olive trees?'

'But they should have been done weeks ago.'

'Yes, we know.'

And that's when we first became acquainted with the Greek version of Harry Enfield's "You don't wanna do it like that", which has frequently accompanied most pieces of advice we've been given since.

'But that's how Pavlos told us to do it,' I said.

'Pavlos? Pah! The man's an idiot. He sells second hand tractors. What does that *maláka* know about pruning olive trees?'

So then he grabbed the pruning saw that Pavlos had

lent us and clambered up into the nearest tree that hadn't yet been seriously maimed by our apparently misguided efforts. Lopping branches this way and that, he moved with jaw-droppingly impressive speed and agility, totally ignoring his father's comments that 'You shouldn't have taken that one out' and 'Why didn't you cut that one?' (Yes, the Greeks are more than happy to inflict the "You don't wanna do it like that" on each other as often as they do on us.)

To be honest, Yiorgos's pruning method didn't seem much unlike Pavlos's, but there were a few subtle differences which we decided we ought to try and adopt ourselves. But a couple of trees later, and yet another local farmer called in.

'You should have pruned those weeks ago.'

'Yes. We know.'

'You don't wanna do it like that.'

As I recall, I think we had about eight different farmers telling us how to prune an olive tree in the space of two days, each one saying that the previous demonstrator of the sacred art was a complete idiot and didn't know a hawk from a pruning saw – or whatever the Greek equivalent is.

Since then, Yiorgos has become our self-appointed Adviser-in-Chief and delights in taking every opportunity to offer advice and/or explain to us in great detail how we're performing a certain task in completely the wrong way. He and his dad have often stopped by on their tractor when they've been on their way to one of their nearby plots of land, and they sometimes come bearing gifts. These usually consist of one or two carrier bags stuffed full of whichever of their produce happens to be in season at the time. We're always grateful for these acts of generosity, of course, but in the spirit of "Beware of Greeks bearing gifts", the downside is that we then have to put up with Yiorgos's latest lecture on

"You don't wanna do it like that".

There was one time when the gift in question was a dozen or so fresh eggs, although Yiorgos seemed to get the impression that we'd never seen an egg before in our lives.

'*Ella*, Robert. *Ella*,' he said, grabbing the bag of eggs back from me and marching purposefully into the house.

He then took a frying pan and put it on the hob, making sure that I was paying close attention as he added some olive oil and lit the flame. Once he was satisfied that the oil was hot enough, he took one of the eggs and broke it into the pan.

'*Vlépeis*?' he said as he gently tilted the pan this way and that. 'You see?'

Naturally, I feigned amazement at this demonstration of Yiorgos's culinary skill, but I couldn't help thinking that this was a new but closely related variation on teaching your grandmother to suck eggs.

* * *

Not dissimilar to the impromptu two-day olive pruning workshop was the occasion when we got the camper van stuck in the mud. This was during our first winter at Xerika, soon after some seriously heavy rain and right in the middle of the olive harvest. We'd been heading into town for essential supplies (e.g. beer and tobacco) when I inadvertently backed the van off the concrete parking area and into nearly a foot of mud. Since the van is rear wheel drive, this was definitely not a good thing to happen. However, because it was the olive harvesting season, there was no shortage of nearby farmers to come and offer their advice – and even practical assistance.

The first arrived within seconds of hearing the first slithery spin of the wheels and recommended the use of an olive net to give the tyres something to grip on. This succeeded only in wrapping a now very muddy olive net round the back axle.

'Netting's no good,' said the next farmer to arrive on the scene. 'You want to use wood.'

I duly obliged with a couple of offcuts, which ended up being rocketed out from under the wheels at such a rate that they could easily have taken someone's head off if they'd been foolish enough to be standing within range.

'Any idiot knows that you need stones for this sort of job,' said Farmer Number Three.

But all the stones did was to sink deeper into the mud as soon as I began to turn the wheels.

By this time, there were six farmers assembled around the van, and not all the same ones who'd advised us on the correct method for pruning olive trees earlier in the year. And whenever two or more Greeks are met together for the express purpose of solving a particular *próblima*, the arguments inevitably become heated to the point of deafening. To be fair, though, there's often as much shouting and arm waving when they're agreeing with each other, so it's sometimes hard to tell whether they're just about to slap each other on the back and adjourn to the nearest taverna or rip each other's throats out.

Every new suggestion for how to get the van out of the mud resulted not only in complete failure and more arguing but also in most of us being coated in yet another layer of reddish-brown gloop. This was especially the case when we all resorted to the brute force method of pushing and shoving at the back of the van, which in turn led to an extended period of head scratching and arguing.

It was eventually agreed that the only solution would be to use a tractor to tow the van out, but amazingly enough, not one of the six farmers had happened to bring theirs with them that day. After another lengthy debate about whose tractor would be best for the job, Andreas gave Kostas Moustaki a lift on his clapped-out old moped to fetch his from the village, which was – and still is – about four kilometres away. (Incidentally, Moustaki isn't his real name. It's just that there are so many Kostas's in Greece that they often have nicknames to distinguish one from the other, and perhaps not surprisingly, this particular Kostas was so nicknamed because of his impressively large Viva Zapata moustache. Rather less charitably, some also referred to him as K-K-K-Kostas because of his occasional stammer.)

Once Kostas had returned with his monster of a tractor, complete with motorised winch, the job of towing the van out of the mud was completed in a matter of minutes. We were so grateful that I didn't even mind when all six farmers formed an orderly queue (unusual in Greece) so they could take their turn to inform me that: 'You don't wanna back the van onto the mud when it's been raining. You wanna keep it on the concrete.' One of them actually accompanied this excellent piece of advice by tapping his forefinger against his temple, which is an internationally recognised gesture for "Use your head next time, you imbecile".

.

10

Thank You, Mr Faraday

One of the aspects of the Greek personality that the "Getting the Van Out of the Mud" episode demonstrates is that Greeks are generally great in an emergency, instantly springing into action regardless of the nature of the emergency and whoever's emergency it might be. At all other times, however, most Greeks will revert to their default setting of *sigá-sigá*. Similar in meaning to the Spanish *mañana*, this translates literally as "slowly-slowly" and is fundamental to the admirable Greek attitude to life of "Why rush to do today what can easily wait till tomorrow – or the day after?"

Outside of an emergency situation, therefore, the successful resolution of any given process will often take much *much* longer than the most patient of mortals would consider reasonable, and this is when the *sigá-sigá* approach can occasionally become somewhat less admirable. I mentioned in an earlier chapter, for instance, that it took eighteen months to get mains electricity to the house after we'd moved in, which rather called into question the estate agent's blurb about Xerika:

"The electricity supply for the house is presently provided by two generators, but it would be easily possible to connect the property to the main power network."

We never did find the second of the two generators,

and I've already gone into more than enough detail about Belching Bertha, so what about the "easily possible" part of connecting mains electricity?

We'd already established that solar power wasn't a realistic option since – surprisingly for a country with wall-to-wall sunshine for most of the year – it was only in the fledgling stage of development in Greece at the time. So, before we signed the contract to buy Xerika, we got a quote from DEH, the public power company, for how much it would cost to link us up to the national grid. The nearest part of the grid was about three kilometres from the house, so we knew it was going to be expensive. But 35,000 euros? There was no way we could afford this on top of what we were already paying for the house and the land, but once the previous owner knew this was a deal breaker, he very generously agreed to pay the vast majority of the thirty-five grand himself.

Papers were signed and stamped, and we were assured that it would be a matter of a few weeks before the product of Michael Faraday's wonderful invention (or was it a discovery?) would be piped into our new home. Belching Bertha's days were numbered – but not, as it turned out, in multiples of seven but rather in multiples of thirty-one. The first problem was that there was a severe shortage of telegraph poles in Greece, and nobody seemed to have any idea when more would be available.

In fact, it was about a year before DEH managed to get hold of enough telegraph poles for the job as they presumably had to wait for the trees they cut them from to grow to the necessary height. Once they'd arrived, though, the speed with which they were put in position was impressive, and the cabling was connected on the same day. But not to the house unfortunately. As far as the gatepost but no further. About half a dozen yards from the house itself. Still, it wouldn't take them long to connect up that last little bit, would it?

Oh yes it would. Our "We're Getting Mains Electricity" celebrations were misguidedly premature, and I began to regret taunting Belching Bertha with her imminent demise when she retaliated by becoming even more temperamental than usual. The old cliché of "so near and yet so far" was never more appropriate as the weeks turned into yet more months of frustration until we decided to raise the matter with the estate agent, who'd set up the whole deal with DEH.

'They're probably waiting for a bribe,' he said in a tone of voice that suggested this was the most natural thing in the world.

For Greek people, the whole culture of *fakeláki* (small brown envelopes containing varying amounts of euros) *is* one of the most natural things in the world. Of course, nobody likes having to bribe a doctor to get themselves higher up the list for a hip operation or bunging a civil servant to get planning permission for their shed, but it's just the way it is in Greece, and it's been like that for decades. So endemic is the *fakeláki* that hardly anyone seems to bat so much as an eyelid whenever they're asked for one. But we're *British*, for goodness' sake. Not for one moment could we condone this sort of behaviour. Absolutely not.

Although…

Well, maybe just this once. I mean, the long-awaited mains electricity was tantalisingly close, and if I had to spend one more day trying to coax Belching Bertha into something that resembled life—

'How much?' I said.

The estate agent gave me one of those typically Greek gestures which involves a shrug and a slight outward turn of the palms. 'Fifty ought to do it.'

'So who do we give it to?'

'Oh, they'll probably make themselves known when they're ready.'

'And when's that likely to be?'

Again the shrug and the palms gesture, and we left the office in search of a shop that sold small brown envelopes.

By a strange coincidence (possibly), we were at home the very next day when we noticed somebody rummaging around in the undergrowth at the side of the track not far from the house. We went to investigate and discovered a middle-aged man in shirt and tie with a clipboard and a pen who seemed to be making detailed notes about the base of one of the telegraph poles. He told us he was from DEH and said he was checking that the contractors had installed everything correctly. When his back was turned, Penny and I exchanged glances of the "Is this the bloke we're supposed to bribe?" variety and then immediately followed these up with Greek-style "How should I know?" shrugs.

'Can we offer you a drink or something?' I said, thinking that if he really was the bloke we were supposed to bribe, he'd accept the offer of hospitality as a precursor to getting his *fakeláki*. At the very least, he might pick up on the "or something" bit as a pretty heavy clue as to what I was actually asking him. After all, we didn't want to bribe the wrong person and then have somebody else turning up the next day and demanding their bunce.

'No thanks,' he said. 'It's getting late, and I need to get home.'

Obviously not the *fakeláki* man… Or was he?

'And you didn't give him the envelope?' said the estate agent the following day when we called into his office and told him what had happened.

'We didn't think he was the right one.'

'Of course he was the right one. You didn't expect him to come right out and ask for it, did you?'

'Well, we haven't exactly had a lot of experience with

this sort of thing.'

'Apparently not,' said the agent with a kind of sniffy disdain that implied this was a serious shortcoming on our part.

Perhaps the *fakeláki* man from DEH had come to the same conclusion himself and decided to give up on his backhander from this couple of idiot Brits because three days later a DEH van pulled up at the gate and had us connected up to our longed-for mains electricity in less than an hour. So, not only had we finally arrived in the twenty-first century, we'd also managed to avoid sacrificing our principles to get there. In celebration, Penny and I spent the next hour or so wasting huge amounts of electricity by switching on various appliances and repeatedly turning light switches on and off for the pure childish thrill of seeing the effect.

I doubt that either of us will ever again take for granted the ease in which it's possible to illuminate a room at the simple flick of a switch, and we're sometimes reminded of the old dark days of the Belching Bertha era by the occasional power cut. Mostly, these are fairly short-lived, but there was one winter when a major thunderstorm knocked out the power for more than twenty-four hours. After the power was eventually restored, we found that the storm had not only destroyed our DVD player but had also severely damaged the electricity meter, which meant that we could use as much electricity as we liked without the meter registering even a tenth of a kilowatt. However, guilt soon got the better of us, but when we asked our electrician how we should go about reporting the fault, his response was something along the lines of: 'Why d'you wanna do that? Let the thieving bastards find out for themselves.' He had a point of course, and we compromised with our guilt by having free electricity for two more days before we owned up.

As for Belching Bertha herself, her services were no longer required after the "Great Switch-On of November 2005", and when Xerika's previous owner asked if he could take her to use in his house on Crete, we didn't hesitate for as much as a nano-second. We did, however, make sure we were out when he came to collect her as I had no desire to get covered in grease, oil, diesel and black soot even for one very last time. Besides, she weighed about a ton, and I value my vertebrae.

11

The "I Bet You Haven't Got X" Gambit

The amount of time it took to get mains electricity to the house is just one example of how nothing is impossible in Greece, but everything is difficult. During our first few months at Xerika, we encountered many more examples, including what we naively assumed would be the perfectly straightforward process of buying a car.

After the incident of the van getting stuck in the mud and the winter rains turning the tracks into the consistency of wet fudge, it soon became apparent that we needed something with four wheel drive if we weren't to be stranded at the house for days at a time. Our initial search for a secondhand four-by-four ended soon after it had begun when we realised that there is almost no understanding of the used car market in Greece. We could, for instance, have had a three year old Suzuki Vitara with thirty-odd thousand kilometres on the clock, but what was the point when we could have bought a brand new one for about a thousand euros more? And it was much the same story at every other dealer we visited. Buying a new car wasn't something we'd budgeted for, but we were left with very little option.

To begin with, we thought that a pickup would be the most sensible choice as we'd need to cart fertiliser sacks and all kinds of other agricultural paraphernalia up from the town at fairly regular intervals:

'Yes, the L200 would be ideal,' said the Mitsubishi salesman. 'The only thing is…'

We'd experienced "the only thing is…" before in Greece, so we waited anxiously for the bombshell to drop.

'…according to Greek law, only people who need a pickup for their work are allowed to buy one. Builders, painters and decorators. That kind of thing.'

'What about farmers?' I said.

'Oh yes, you'd certainly qualify as farmers. The only thing is…'

Here we go again.

'…you'll need quite a lot of documents to support your claim.'

Amongst plenty of others, these turned out to be a residence permit and a certificate to prove we earned at least some of our income from farming. We'd also need to take out health insurance with the Agricultural Insurance Organisation (*Organismós Georgikón Asfalíseon*, or OGA for short).

'So what papers would we need if we bought one of those then?' I said, pointing to a four-by-four Mitsubishi which looked almost identical to the pickup but without the flatbed at the back.

'Just the residence permit,' said the salesman.

'But the only difference is the *shape*.'

We were treated to a Greek palms-spread shrug and a sheepish grin. 'Yes, I know. Crazy, isn't it?'

In the end, we went for the four-by-four without the flatbed – the Pajero Pinin – not because of the hassle of getting all the extra documents but because the back seats of the pickup were seriously uncomfortable. Besides, one of the reviews we'd read said that the Pajero was "boringly reliable", which was absolutely fine by us, given that we'd be driving it up and down a mountain several times a week. First of all, though, we had to get our residence permits from the local police station, which again should have been a perfectly simple operation but wasn't.

When we arrived, there was a small group of cops and ancillary staff hanging round the reception desk having a good old chat.

'*Nai*?' said one of the officers when he finally deigned to register our presence.

'We need residence permits,' I said.

'Why?'

'Because we want to buy a car.'

This was greeted with several pairs of rolling eyeballs and some mutterings about "Have they *still* not changed that stupid law?"

It was patently obvious that none of them wanted any part of what later transpired to be a mammoth form-filling and rubber-stamping exercise even by Greek standards, so they tried the now familiar "I Bet You Haven't Got X" gambit.

'Have you got your passports with you?'

'Yes.'

'Two passport sized photos each?'

'Yes.'

'Tax identification numbers?'

'Yes.'

'House purchase contract?'

'Yes.'

'Proof of parents' inside leg measurements?'

Okay, I made the last one up, but the list of required documents went on and on, the inquisitor becoming increasingly desperate to hit upon something we *didn't* have with us so he could say, 'Aha! We can't deal with you now then. You'll have to come back when you've got it.' This would very possibly have been followed by a group high five, but on this occasion it wasn't to be.

We'd been caught out by the "I Bet You Haven't Got X" gambit before, so we were now in the habit of taking with us a large carrier bag stuffed with every document we possessed whenever we had to deal with any kind of officialdom.

Having finally exhausted his list, the police officer resorted to Plan B. 'It's nearly two o'clock. You'll have to come back tomorrow morning.'

We dutifully obeyed (he was a police officer after all), and when we arrived back at the police station the next day, there was a gang of decorators repainting the inside of the building. I only mention this because they'd finished the whole job in less time than it took to process our residence permits – a little over four hours. Still, at least we finally had our official permission to buy a car, and off we went back to the Mitsubishi dealer to close the deal. This was when we discovered we'd have to wait to get the number plates because there was a national shortage of the metal they're made from. Memories of the shortage of telegraph poles for our mains electricity came flooding back of course, but to be fair, a lot of people were buying new cars around that time as the government had recently, and quite drastically, reduced the purchase tax on them.

When the number plate manufacturers caught up with the backlog a few weeks later, we went to the vehicle licensing office in Kalamata to pick them up. But after we handed in the relevant papers for the car, we were given two long thin number plates instead of one long thin one for the front and a square one for the back. I explained that the plates were for a *tzeep* (jeep) and there wasn't room for a long thin one on the back, only to be told that they'd stopped making the square ones and only produced the long thin ones now.

Clearly, there didn't seem to be much point in debating the matter, so instead we gave the guy the papers for a quad bike (ATV), which we also needed licence plates for. More accurately, we only needed one for the back, and it was a bit of an eyebrow raiser when we were presented with a *square* one which was exactly the same size as the one we should have had for the car.

'But I thought you said...' I started to say but tailed off when I realised that further discussion would be utterly pointless.

After we left the licensing office, we called in at the Mitsubishi dealer to see if Stavros, the manager, had any bright ideas how to solve the number plate problem for the car.

'Yes, we've had a lot of these lately,' he said. 'They don't make the square ones any more.'

'Well, they do,' I said, 'because we've just got one for a quad bike.'

'Ah, but that's a totally different vehicle altogether,' said Stavros as if this was a perfectly logical explanation. 'But don't worry. We can fix this easily.'

I asked if the solution was to cut the long thin plate in two and then mount one half above the other to form a kind of square.

Stavros threw up his hands in horror. 'No, no, no. It's government property. Tampering with a number plate is a criminal offence.'

Then he summoned Christos, the head mechanic. 'Wait till you see him work his magic.'

We watched in awed expectation as Christos took the long thin number plate and brandished it momentarily as if he really was about to perform a conjuring trick. All that was missing was a drum roll, but we were somewhat disappointed when he simply picked up a screwdriver and fixed the plate in the appropriate position on the back of the car.

Distinctly underwhelmed though I was, I didn't want to hurt Christos's feelings, but I nevertheless felt the need to point out that the plate was partially obscuring the left side brake light.

'Wait,' said Stavros. 'He hasn't done the magic part yet.'

Taking his cue, Christos took hold of the overlapping three inches of number plate and bent it towards him through an angle of about thirty degrees so that the brake light was now visible. For good measure, he then applied the same technique to the other end, presumably for no other reason than a slavish devotion to symmetry.

'Brilliant,' I said.

'Amazing,' said Penny.

Christos apparently didn't do sarcasm or just hadn't picked it up in our tones because he simply beamed at us with an expression of such pride it was as if he really had pulled off a feat of magic so astonishing it would have made Derren Brown look like a fumbling amateur.

12

Whose Gas Is It Anyway?

The hassles involved in what should have been the simple process of buying a car demonstrated once again that nothing is impossible in Greece, but everything is difficult. Compared to the UK, though, where a lot of things are difficult and quite a few things are utterly impossible, this might seem to be not a bad trade-off. However, the absurd amounts of bureaucracy and red tape in Greece are at least partly responsible for the dire financial mess the country is in today. Take, for example, the obstacles involved in starting up a new business.

There was one guy I read about recently who wanted to start a business selling olive products online. It took him ten months to get all the official paperwork sorted out, and the banks weren't much help either. He approached three different ones for help in processing online payments, and although the guy explained that the main purpose was to *export* his products, all of them insisted that certain sections of his website – including the marketing and privacy policies – had to be written *exclusively* in Greek and no other language at all. But the real hoot about this story was that even though this was to be an entirely web-based company, it would still be selling food products, so each member of the board had to submit not only lung X-rays but stool samples as well.

From our own experiences, there's a fair bit of

incompetence that goes with all the bureaucracy, which is probably another reason why some Greek businesses and organisations have been losing money hand over fist. Take OGA, for instance. This is the pensions and health insurance wing of the Greek farmers' union, which we subscribe to ourselves and which is in serious financial trouble, partly because only about 62% of its members are paying their contributions. This may well be explained by the fact that people just can't afford to pay their subscriptions any more, but if our own experience is anything to go by, it's also down to OGA's incompetence.

We're supposed to get billed every six months, but when we actually receive the bills is a different matter altogether. Because our house is so remote, we don't get our mail delivered but have a PO Box in the local post office, which we check about once a week. (Xerika's remoteness also explains why our electricity meter is only read every three years or so and why it's impossible to get pizza delivered.) Despite having repeatedly told OGA what our PO Box number was since the day we joined, it took seven years before they finally got round to typing the three little digits into their computer. Until then, the bills either turned up at a local taverna or in one of the bulging boxes of undelivered mail in the post office, and we just had to wade through them until we found our OGA bill. I should also mention here that about 70% of the letters in these boxes were bills from OGA, most of which probably ended up not being paid. No wonder OGA is in deep financial trouble when they make it so difficult for people to pay their contributions even when they want to.

While I'm on the subject of OGA, here's something else which makes it difficult for people to pay their contributions, although ELTA (the Greek postal service) has to accept responsibility for this one rather than OGA itself. Since capital controls were introduced here in June 2015, the amount of cash that could be withdrawn from a Greek bank account has been strictly limited – currently to 420 euros per week. This has meant that more and more people have been using credit and debit cards to pay for stuff, which suits the government rather well because it's had a major effect on the previously rampant "grey economy".

When we first came to Greece, we were amazed at how few people paid for anything with plastic compared to the UK. During all the years before capital controls were introduced, I don't remember seeing more than a handful of Greeks paying with anything but cash at supermarkets, petrol stations, etcetera, and many of them would peel off the required note or two from a thick wad of what must have been a thousand euros or more. Plumbers, electricians and so on were also paid in cash, and this of course meant that the state was missing out on huge sums in direct and indirect taxes. As for the Athens dentist who declared his annual income to be fourteen hundred euros, I can only imagine that he must have had a seriously bad reputation for butchery amongst his prospective clientele.

Prior to the sudden upsurge in the use of credit and debit cards, I'm not even sure that many supermarkets or petrol stations actually had the equipment necessary to process them, but now almost everybody has it – except, apparently, our local post office. Towards the end of last year, we had to pay our biannual bill for OGA health insurance, which came to 440 euros, so off we went to the post office and joined the end of the lengthy queue of OGA members who'd also chosen to pay up on the last possible day before a fine would be imposed.

As we waited, we were a little surprised to notice that everyone in front of us was paying in cash, but we assumed that most of them were probably farmers, who

– in this area at least – are notoriously reluctant to accept anything new, such as an invention-of-the-devil piece of plastic that was going to rob them of their entire life savings if they were ever foolhardy enough to sign up for one. However, when it came to our turn, we handed over our OGA bill and waved our debit card at the woman behind the counter.

'I'm sorry,' she said, 'but we don't take plastic.'

'But this is the post office,' I said, 'and you're owned by the state, which for the past several months has been telling everyone to use cards instead of cash.'

The woman shrugged. 'Not here, you can't.'

'Not only that,' I added, 'but ELTA is also a bank, isn't it?'

'Kind of,' she said. 'And that's why we've got a cash machine just outside the main door, so might I suggest you use your debit card in that to withdraw the cash and then come back here to pay your bill?'

By the time we'd done that and rejoined the end of the queue, it now extended out of the door and almost reached the cash machine itself. Fortunately, we managed to scrape together the additional twenty euros we needed on top of the four hundred and twenty maximum we could withdraw, although this left us with only a pocketful of change to last us for the next seven days.

To set the record straight, though, I'm not suggesting that bureaucracy or incompetence are exclusive to Greece alone. Certainly not. I've got plenty of examples from the UK, and one that immediately springs to mind is British Gas. Some years before we came to Greece, I'd just moved in to a rented house, and the landlady said I should phone all the utility companies and get them to change the accounts to my name. I started with British Gas, and after the usual annoying menu system – "Press nine if you want someone to come round and help you tear your own head off" – I finally got through to what could loosely be described as a human being. I explained what I wanted to do, and there was a couple of minutes' keyboard tapping before the gas woman came back with: 'I'm sorry, sir, but we don't supply gas to that address.'

'I think you do,' I said.

'Not according to our records we don't.'

'Well, your records must be wrong then.'

'I don't think so, sir,' said the woman, clearly affronted by my temerity in daring to question the efficiency of her beloved corporation.

'Look, I've got your last bill right here in front of me,' I said. I've just read the account number to you.'

I seem to remember that I held the bill up to the mouthpiece of the phone for additional, although ultimately pointless, emphasis.

'Does it say "British Gas" at the top?' she said.

'Ooh, wait a minute. Let me see. Buh – ruh – ih – tuh – Yes, definitely British Gas.'

'Well, I don't know where that came from then because we don't supply gas to that address.'

I gasped in feigned horror. 'What? You don't mean you think the bill is... a forgery?'

In the end, I even resorted to turning up one of the burners on the gas cooker full blast and holding the phone up to it.

'Do you hear that noise?' I said. 'That's gas, that is.'

'That's as may be, sir, but how do I know you're actually at the address in question. You could be in another house altogether.'

'Oh for f—'

'Besides,' said the gas woman, 'even if you *are* at the address in question, it's definitely not our gas.'

'You can tell that just from the sound, can you? Amazing.'

This particular example of institutionalised

incompetence did eventually get sorted out, and the only reason I persisted was that I didn't want to end up with a massive bill one day when British Gas finally cottoned on and rang me with a: 'You know when we told you six years ago that we didn't supply gas to that address?'

At least we get our gas out of bottles in Greece.

13

A Very Berry Christmas

Of all the advice we'd gleaned from our research into moving abroad before we came to Greece, some of the daftest was to be found on the subject of healthcare. For example, in at least one of the books we read, we were advised that it was essential to take our medical records with us as well as our dental and optical records. We dismissed the latter two as being a daft idea as any optician or dentist you visit for the first time is bound to do their own checkups, but taking our medical records seemed fairly sensible at the time. Well, it did to me anyway. Penny thought this was also a daft idea, but then she doesn't have my deep-seated propensity for hypochondria.

The receptionist at our local GP's surgery in England also seemed to think this was a daft idea but didn't try too hard to dissuade me as she presumably saw this as an opportunity to make a bit of extra cash for the practice. Thirty quid in "administrative and photocopying fees" for an envelope stuffed full of sheets of paper, about a quarter of which were blank. And the writing on those that weren't blank was so illegible as to be utterly useless even to a doctor trained in the art of indecipherable scribbling – especially one whose first language wasn't English. Not that I've ever put it to the test. So far, touch wood (I'm superstitious as well as hypochondriac), the need hasn't arisen since our only dealings with the Greek health services have been for relatively minor health issues. These included a visit to a local gynaecologist when Penny needed a routine checkup.

I would have been quite happy to have stayed where I was in the waiting room, but for some reason the gynaecologist insisted that I came too when he called Penny into his surgery. While Penny "assumed the position" on the examination table with her feet up in stirrups, I hovered in the corner of the room and studied a particularly fascinating piece of flaking paint on the wall. That was until…

'Here, come and have a look at this,' said the gynaecologist with what seemed to me to be a rather inappropriate hint of excitement in his voice. On the other hand, his upbeat tone reassured me that he hadn't actually discovered anything wrong.

Reluctant to abandon my detailed study of the flaking paintwork, I stayed where I was and glanced cautiously over my shoulder. The gynaecologist was crouching down in front of the relevant area of Penny's anatomy and giving it a thorough inspection with the aid of a pen torch.

He was beckoning me with his free hand. 'Hurry up. I haven't got all day.'

I resisted the temptation to say something dismissive along the lines of 'It's okay, I've seen it before' and resume my own, less anatomical examination of the wall, but it appeared that I didn't have much choice in the matter, so I sidled over as if approaching the edge of a very high clifftop.

'There,' said the gynaecologist. 'You see?'

I didn't, to be honest, but mainly because I wasn't really looking. Still, I made the sort of noises of astonishment that seemed to be expected, and apparently satisfied with my response, he switched off his torch, pulled himself upright and pronounced that all was as it should be. We paid and left the surgery in a hurry to find the nearest bar. I needed a drink almost as much as Penny did after her ordeal.

'Look, I'm sorry about that,' I said. 'I mean, I didn't exactly have a lot of choice.'

She shrugged. 'What's to be sorry about?'

'Well, wasn't it a bit... you know... humiliating?'

'Not particularly,' she said. 'But I must admit I was a bit concerned he was about to call in the rest of the waiting room to have a good gawp.'

While I'm on the rather delicate subject of matters gynaecological, I may as well mention a related incident which involved an English friend of ours who lives near the same town. Before she came to Greece, she'd been having treatment for something amiss in the ladies' front-bottom department and needed to continue it once she was here, so she sought out a local GP.

'That's very interesting,' said the nice man in the white coat who'd listened patiently for the best part of three minutes while Melanie (not her real name) explained in intimate detail the exact nature of her problem, 'but I'm actually a dentist.'

It's understandable that Melanie mistook the dentist's surgery for the gynaecologist's for a number of reasons. The healthcare system in Greece is quite different from Britain in that each town will have one or two general practices but also several specialists with their own practices. It's quite a good idea really since most people know whether they have a back problem, an ear nose and throat problem, or whatever it might be, so they can skip the GP stage altogether and go straight to the specialist they need to consult.

In Kyparissia, there are probably about twenty separate practices, each of which is identified with the same sign outside – a red cross on a white background.

Since Melanie had only been in the country for a few days and didn't know the system, she assumed that there were an awful lot of GPs for such a small town and just picked one at random. And because she didn't speak any Greek – never mind read it – she was also unaware that the words underneath the red cross were there to indicate, for example, whether the surgery was a dentist's or a doctor's. Her mistake was therefore not surprising, but what *is* odd is that the dentist she spoke to listened intently for so long while she described her gynaecological problems in great detail and never once interrupted her to tell her she was in the wrong place. But perhaps this is simply another example of the inquisitive nature of most Greeks, who are always keen to find out everything about you and your life, which – according to Melanie's experience at least – apparently includes the kind of information you probably wouldn't even tell your own mother.

And here's another cultural generalisation. A lot of Greeks avoid going to the doctor if at all possible, which seems to be a result of their tendency towards the "If it ain't broke, don't fix it" attitude to life. Fair enough in some ways, but this kind of "cure is better than prevention" approach does have its disadvantages. For instance, it's easy enough to buy all kinds of ointments and lotions for *after* you've been bitten by a mosquito and almost impossible to find anything that's designed to stop you being bitten in the first place.

Similarly, the concept of having your car serviced appears to most Greek people as being unnecessarily pessimistic. I discovered this at first hand when I took the camper van to the local garage a few days before we were due to drive to the UK for our first return visit.

'What's wrong with it?' said the mechanic.

'Nothing as far as I know,' I said. 'It's just that we're going on a long trip soon, so I thought it would be a good idea to give it a service.'

'A what?'

'A service,' I repeated, knowing full well that this wasn't a linguistic failure of communication because "service" is exactly the same in Greek, albeit with a slight difference in pronunciation.

The mechanic thought about it for several moments and then said, 'Change the oil?'

'That sort of thing, yes.'

'New oil filter?'

'Yep.'

He then listed very nearly every single item that would have appeared on the checklist for a standard car service, pausing each time for me to confirm that this was indeed something else I wanted him to do. He didn't do a bad job either, except he did manage to break the accelerator pedal as I discovered when I tried to drive away from the garage.

But back to the Greek healthcare system. As I said earlier, Penny and I haven't needed to put it to the test for anything serious so far, but we've been generally impressed on the few occasions we've had to visit the local hospital. Our most recent experience was a year ago when a friend needed an operation to repair a broken hip. It's a system in Greece – and a very good one, I think – that whenever someone has to have an operation, three of their relatives or friends are required to donate blood before the surgeon will even pick up their scalpel. The blood group doesn't have to be the same as the patient's, and the surgery may not even need a blood transfusion. It's just a way of keeping the blood banks topped up.

'That's fine,' said Penny when Tom's wife Nuala phoned and asked if we could spare some of the red stuff. 'When do you need it?'

'Soon as you can,' said Nuala. 'The operation's this

afternoon.'

So off we went to the hospital with another friend, Pat, and I was under strict instructions from Penny to curb my natural instinct to quote from Tony Hancock's *Blood Donor* sketch (e.g. "A pint? That's very nearly an armful.")

As it turned out, though, they didn't want my or Penny's blood at all. Pat's was fine, but Penny's blood pressure was too high, and my blood test showed that I had some kind of infection. Rather worrying, of course – especially Penny's blood pressure – but what was really impressive was that one of the blood donation staff rushed us both down to the outpatients' clinic almost immediately, and we were given a thorough going over by three different doctors. A remarkably swift and efficient response considering neither of us were emergency cases or even members of the Royal Family.

Other people we know have also generally had good experiences, and one example is the young British couple who whisked their two year old daughter to the hospital after they'd spotted her eating some of the berries off their Christmas tree. (A proper living one and not a plastic imitation job.) They'd taken a handful of the berries with them to show the doctor, and after they explained what had happened, he examined them carefully and said, 'And you're sure that these are the same kind of berries that your daughter ate?'

'Yes, absolutely,' said the even more anxious parents.

The doctor glanced up at them, then swallowed the whole lot and said, 'Very nice. Your kid will be fine.'

Now that's what I call positive reassurance.

Another good thing about healthcare in Greece is you can often avoid a visit to the doctor by going direct to a pharmacy instead. You can buy a lot more medicines over the counter here than you can in Britain, so for instance, there's no need for a prescription if you want antibiotics. You can even go to a pharmacy for a tetanus injection and various other jabs, but you sometimes have to be prepared to drop your trousers in front of a shop full of people.

When we first came to Greece and our command of the language was little more than rudimentary, it was also a relief to discover that most pharmacists speak English. On one occasion, however, I needed some travel sickness tablets, but the pharmacist didn't know more than a couple of words of English, and I certainly didn't know what "travel sickness" was in Greek. Miming the "travel" part was relatively easy, and the pharmacist quickly picked up that I was pretending to drive a car. Conveying the "sickness" bit was a little trickier, though, but not nearly as difficult as the time when one of our visitors wanted me to get her some haemorrhoid ointment.

On a more serious note, Greece's health system has suffered badly because of the austerity measures introduced since the beginning of the economic crisis with some hospitals being closed completely and others being downgraded to provide outpatient care only. Thousands of hospital employees have lost their jobs or have moved abroad in search of better pay and conditions, while those who remain are having to work much longer hours for up to 40% less wages. There is a shortage of essential medical equipment, and many Greeks have lost their entitlement to free healthcare, partly because the rapidly growing number of unemployed people lose their right to free medicines and treatment after one year.

Understandably, there have been major protests about the effects that austerity measures have had on the Greek health service, and in one incident, doctors at the biggest state hospital in Athens made their objections clear by covering the front wall with blood. I dread to think what the sewage workers might do if they decide to hold a protest.

14

May Contain Words

In an earlier chapter, I mentioned the man we bought our fridge from and how he delivered the cooker hob and gas bottle at the same time even though we'd bought these from a different shop. But that was only part of the story. In fact, it was only through sheer luck, or possibly some kind of miracle, that we were still sufficiently in one piece to be able to buy the fridge at all.

Before we'd set off on our quest for the cooker, we'd asked a British couple who lived locally where would be the best place to start.

'Tacky shop is probably your best bet,' they'd said.

We weren't convinced how wise it was to buy something like a cooker from a shop that had a reputation for selling tacky goods, but we obediently followed their detailed directions and arrived at one of those Aladdin's cave type emporiums you can find in every Greek town but which are now sadly lacking in the UK.

There was everything from toilet brushes to teapots, tablecloths to barbecue sets, and an impressive range of olive harvesting equipment. Despite our concerns, though, there was hardly anything that seemed in the least bit tacky. The shopkeeper was one of those people whose default facial expression appeared to be a broad smile, and he painstakingly explained the relative merits – or otherwise – of the various cooker hobs he had on display. We eventually decided on a brown metal one with two main burners and a much smaller one in the middle which, as far as we could tell, is designed exclusively for the miniature aluminium saucepans (*bríkıa*) people use for making Greek coffee.

Having established that we also needed a gas bottle to go with it, the shopkeeper volunteered to fit one for us and check that everything was working properly. A straightforward enough procedure, but once he'd connected the rubber tube from the hob to a ten-kilo bottle of butane gas, he then pulled a cigarette lighter from his pocket and held it up to the seal at the gas end.

'Um,' I said as Penny and I took a step backwards, both of us having guessed what he was about to do. 'What's the er... lighter for?'

His smile faded by a fraction of a wrinkle as he stared up at me with one of those "Don't tell me you never do this in England" looks and said, 'To test that there's no gas escaping of course.'

'I see,' I said as Penny and I both took another step back. 'But what if the gas *is* escaping?'

His smile not only returned but transformed itself into an enormous grin of almost manic proportions. 'Then... *boom*!' he said, throwing his hands in the air as if additional emphasis were needed, and without a moment's pause, fired up the lighter and presumably ran the flame around the entire circumference of the seal.

I say "presumably" because I'd rather pointlessly closed my eyes by then and only opened them again after the anticipated explosion failed to materialise.

'You see?' said the shopkeeper. 'No "boom".'

'Great,' I said and followed him to the cash desk, my hands trembling as I reached in my pocket for the necessary euros.

But just as he was handing me my change, a woman appeared at the back of the shop and called out, 'Lunch is ready, Taki. Are you closing up now?'

'Taki?' I repeated.

The shopkeeper's smile eased into a slight frown of mild bemusement. 'Taki, yes. It's my name.'

So that explained why most of the stuff in *Taki's shop* didn't seem tacky at all (although the pink plastic cruet set was definitely borderline), and we've been regular customers of his ever since. We even buy our refill gas bottles from him, but after that first time, we've always fitted them to the cooker hob ourselves and done our own seal testing – without the aid of a naked flame.

This was one of our earliest experiences of a fairly widespread disregard for health and safety in Greece, but we've come across it many times since. About a year after the potentially catastrophic gas bottle incident, for instance, we were about to set off for a brief visit back to the UK in our elderly camper van when it developed a serious engine fault. We were already booked on the Greece-Italy ferry the following day, so getting the problem fixed was something of an emergency.

When we coaxed the van into his garage and explained the urgent need to repair the fault, Dimitris – known to everyone as Jimmy – proved himself to be no exception to the general rule that most Greeks are great in an emergency. He immediately dropped what he was working on, opened the engine compartment at the back of the van and identified the problem in less than a couple of minutes. Even if he'd explained it in English, I doubt we'd have had any better idea what his diagnosis was, but it did appear that he could make a temporary repair which would at least get us to England and back.

The next moment, he went and fetched his industrial-sized welding equipment and lit the flame. Not having a clue what the Greek was for "Er, do you not think it would be advisable to drain the petrol tank *before* you do that?", I then realised that Penny was still inside the van and talking to somebody on her mobile.

'You might want to come out of there now,' I said, speaking as calmly as possible so as not to create unnecessary alarm.

'I'm on the phone,' she silently mouthed back at me and carried on with her conversation.

Having failed with the softly-softly, no-need-to-panic approach and noticing that Jimmy's head and shoulders and his welding torch had already disappeared inside the engine compartment, I decided that creating alarm was now *absolutely* necessary.

'Get out of the van. Now!'

This was met with a look that I easily interpreted as "Which bit of my silently mouthed 'I'm on the phone' did you not understand?", so I added, 'Or do you want to be burned to death in the massive explosion that's about to happen at any moment?'

The desired effect achieved at last, Penny jumped out of the van, spotted what Jimmy was up to, and we both retreated to an area where we might escape the blast with only some minor cuts and abrasions. Ten minutes later, however, Jimmy's head emerged from inside the engine compartment.

'Done,' he said with a beaming smile and, to our great relief, extinguished the flame of the welding torch.

And so we had survived our second near-death experience of an explosive nature, although both of these were relatively insignificant compared to an incident a couple of years ago which could have destroyed half of Raches, one of our nearest villages. During the Second World War when Greece was occupied by the Nazis, one of the tactics used by the resistance fighters was to steal whatever guns and other military equipment they could from the Germans. On one such occasion, a group from Raches managed to deprive the occupying forces of a not insubstantial sized bomb, and one of their members volunteered to hide it under the stairs in his house. Unfortunately, however, he then forgot all about it, and there it remained under the stairs until his granddaughter came across it while she happened to be doing some long overdue "de-cluttering".

The police were duly summoned, and they in turn called in a bomb disposal squad, who safely defused the device and carted it away. It was the most exciting thing to have happened in the village for years – possibly decades – and the event was talked about for weeks afterwards, but at least the *whole* village was still alive to tell the tale and not just half of it.

The very fact that someone could actually *forget* they had a bomb under their stairs is perhaps another indication of most Greek people's indifferent attitude to health and safety. Conversely, the British are generally a great deal more mindful of health and safety issues, although the vast majority now believe that we've reached the point of "health and safety gone mad". No-one is credited with having so much as an ounce of common sense any more, which is why almost any product you buy – especially anything electrical – comes complete with an inch-thick manual, three-quarters of which is filled with safety warnings such as "Do not use while sleeping" (hairdryer) and "Do not use underwater" (electric toaster). Both of these are real examples and so too are the following warning labels:

- "This product may contain residue of nuts" (packet of cashew nut pieces);
- "May cause drowsiness" (Nytol sleeping aid);
- "Keep away from children" (baby lotion);
- "Do not attempt to swallow" (mattress).

Only recently, we bought a pair of nail scissors when we were in the UK, and on the back of the packaging were a variety of warnings including "For external use only", so at least the manufacturer is doing its bit to reduce waiting times at Accident and Emergency departments. But underneath, it also said "Suitable for diabetics". I mean, how confusing is that? Do they mean it's only safe to swallow an entire pair of nail scissors if you happen to be diabetic?

I'm not by any means a subscriber to the Darwinian "survival of the fittest" philosophy, but if anyone's stupid enough to try and eat a pair of nail scissors or use a toaster while it's submerged in a bath full of water, they probably deserve to die anyway. Harsh, I know, but I'm sure most of us have a lot more common sense than we're given credit for. On the other hand, if we continue to be treated like idiots, maybe evolution will eventually deprive us of common sense altogether and we really will end up trying to swallow mattresses.

* * *

During the Second World War, on 28th October 1940, Mussolini demanded free access into Greece for his troops, but the Greek response was quite simple: "*Ochi*" – "No". Since then, 28th October has become one of the most important dates in the Greek calendar, and there are major festivities to commemorate "Ochι Day". Consequently, in a country which actually *celebrates* the very act of saying "No", if the Greek authorities followed Britain's overly zealous example and tried to introduce a whole range of new health and safety regulations, it probably wouldn't make the slightest difference. For one thing, the cavalier attitude to health and safety in Greece seems to be as innate as the relaxed approach to life in general, and for another, Greek people are fiercely resistant to being told what they can and can't do. So much so that I can almost imagine some of them wading through the safety warnings in the previously mentioned product manuals just so they knew what it is that they have to disobey – 'Effi, it says here that you're not supposed to operate this chainsaw while under the influence of alcohol. Well, sod that for a game of soldiers. Pass me that ouzo bottle.'

In Greece, almost all laws and regulations are considered to be gross infringements of the individual's right to do whatever he or she damn well pleases. Nor is the Greek government itself immune from this kind of attitude, with successive administrations regularly flouting many of the rules and regulations handed down by the European Union. Take the ban on smoking in enclosed public places, for example, which was introduced in Greece in September 2010. For the first three or four months, this was enforced without much enthusiasm by the authorities, and a few taverna owners were fined for allowing customers to light up on their premises. Since then, however, it's as if the ban on smoking was purely a figment of everyone's imagination because it seemed to vanish almost overnight in, well... a puff of smoke.

Nowadays, it's back to business as usual with people getting their nicotine fixes pretty much anywhere they like. And with what I like to think was a neat piece of irony, a Greek-owned ferry we were travelling on a couple of years ago had glass ashtrays with a large no-smoking symbol emblazoned across its base in bright red. But deliberately ironic or not, it certainly seemed to epitomise the barely even lip-service compliance with rules and regulations.

As a shamefaced smoker myself – but hopefully one who is considerate of others – I don't really have a problem with people being able to light up in public places *outdoors*. On the other hand, I would wholeheartedly back any legislation which seriously discouraged service station attendants from smoking while filling a car with petrol – especially when I'm next in the queue and well within the potential blast range.

And if by some miracle the service station shop hasn't been totally obliterated by the massive explosion, you can pop in and buy a handy little gadget that prevents the annoying alarm going off in your car when you haven't fastened your seat belt. This consists of a piece of plastic in the shape of a seat belt clip that you simply slot into the buckle to fool the alarm system into believing that you're securely strapped into your seat. These little plastic gizmos are not only sold at service stations but in various other shops as well, and as far as I'm aware, they're not even illegal.

Motorcyclists wearing crash helmets – or rather, not wearing them – is another example of how Greek people resent being told what they can and can't do. Although most riders of the bigger bikes do seem to comply with this particular law these days, it wasn't at all uncommon when we first moved to Greece to see motorcyclists hurtle past us on bikes with only marginally less power than a NASA space rocket wearing nothing more than T-shirts, shorts and flip-flops – and sometimes, for the men at least, not even the T-shirts.

It was only after witnessing many other examples of the Greek love affair with ignoring all things regulatory that I began to develop a theory that if the authorities really did want to enforce some law or other, a bit of reverse psychology would almost certainly do the trick. Something along the lines of: "The wearing of crash helmets whilst riding a motorcycle is strictly forbidden." – 'You what? Think you lot can tell me what I can and can't do, eh? Effi! Fetch me that bike helmet.'

15

Crimes and Misdemeanours and a Little Piece of Plastic

In contrast to the majority of the Greek population, it's probably fair to say that most Brits have some kind of innate aversion to disobeying rules. That "Keep Off The Grass" sign must be there for a reason. And what about those pelican crossings? Very few of us would *dream* of setting foot on one until the little red person turns green, even when the road is clear for a mile in either direction.

Most Brits even obey rules that aren't really rules at all. Take queueing, for instance. Without wishing to boast, I think it's universally acknowledged that the British are the best queuers in the world, waiting patiently in line until it's our turn to be served with whatever it is we want to be served with. There are probably even quite a number of Brits who see a "Please Queue Here" sign outside a cinema and automatically stop in front of it despite having absolutely no intention of going in to watch the film.

Like many British people – and certainly those of my generation – I was brought up to follow rules slavishly and to abide by the law, although I did once receive a somewhat mixed message when I was about nine years old and from what I considered to be a rather surprising source. Her name was Miss Dixon, and she was a teacher with a deservedly fierce reputation for not suffering rule-breakers lightly. The surprise, therefore, was when I overheard her talking to another teacher and giving her opinion that 'There must be something wrong with any child who goes through this school without ever having had a detention.' (For those who are unfamiliar with the term, a detention is when you're made to stay behind after school – usually for an hour – and carry out some completely pointless task like writing out "I must not draw unflattering pictures of Mr Battersby on the blackboard" several hundred times over.)

During the year and a bit that I'd already been at the school, I'd scrupulously avoided breaking any of the rules, however absurd I might have thought them to be, and I was now deeply worried that, according to Miss Dixon, there might be something wrong with me. So, determined to dispel the fear that I might not be "normal", I immediately set about getting myself a detention. Not that this was at all difficult as I simply waited until I was sure Miss Dixon herself was watching and then brazenly marched five paces into an area known as "out of bounds" (i.e. beyond the perimeter of the school grounds). And hey presto, after an hour's detention and a few hundred "I must not venture out of bounds during school hours", I had proved to myself – and Miss Dixon – that there was nothing wrong with me after all. Such was my relief that when I got home and my mother asked me why I was late, I proudly announced with a beaming smile that I'd been in detention – just in case my parents had also been thinking there was something wrong with me.

My fledgling crime spree didn't end there, though, because in the summer of that same year, I committed a robbery that still pricks my conscience even now. My parents had taken my brother and I on holiday to South Wales (for the third year running) and on the very first day bought me a toy tuna fishing boat, which I played with incessantly in the shallows of the traditionally cold, grey sea. But this wasn't any old toy tuna fishing boat. Oh no. This one had all sorts of detachable bits and pieces in garishly coloured plastic – seats, helm, cabin door, pointy platform thing at the bow – but so much rough handling did it get that two of the bits and pieces inevitably detached themselves and were swept away, never to be seen again.

I was understandably distraught that my boat was no longer fully seaworthy without a helm and one of its orange radio antennae, so when we went to another toyshop a couple of days later, my eyes lit up at the sight of about two dozen identical boats in a jumbled heap in a corner of the floor. I was obviously stricken with a serious moral dilemma, but when I investigated more closely, I discovered that several of the detachable bits and pieces were littered here and there amongst the heap. Clearly, as I convinced myself at the time, they were surplus to requirements. So, making sure on this occasion that no-one was watching, into my pocket went a brand new helm and an orange antenna.

Once back outside the shop, the pounding in my chest began to subside, although my relief at having successfully pulled off the heist was marred by a growing sense of guilt. But worse was yet to come. Much worse. No sooner had we all got into the car than my father turned on the radio and, this being a Sunday morning, slap in the middle of a *Morning Service* broadcast. The congregation was just finishing off the last rousing chorus of *Onward Christian Soldiers*, and the next thing I heard was the priest beginning his sermon with the words: 'My text for today will be the eighth commandment – Thou shalt not steal.'

Was this a complete coincidence or some kind of divine intervention? Had God (being omniscient) just watched me nicking the tuna fishing boat parts and (being omnipotent) managed to get the priest to change the originally planned subject of his sermon? But coincidence or not, I immediately broke into a sweat, and the pounding started up again in my chest, the tempo rapidly increasing as the priest explained in graphic detail the horrific fate that awaited anyone who dared to break the eighth commandment. Eternal damnation, fire and brimstone – the whole hellish kit and caboodle. And although he didn't specifically *mention* detachable bits and pieces from a toy tuna fishing boat, I fully believed in all that hellfire stuff as an impressionable nine-year-old, so I was utterly convinced that this terrifyingly dire warning was aimed directly at me.

I daren't tell my parents what I'd done, so returning the plastic helm and antenna to the shop clearly wasn't an option. Dropping them, unseen by earthly mortals, into the nearest litter bin as soon as we got out of the car was, though, so that's what I did. My hope was that not benefiting from the spoils of my heinous crime and making do with a helmless and single-antennaed tuna fishing boat for the rest of the holiday might at least be seen as mitigation. In which case, I'd surely get the occasional timeout from the roasting fires of Hell that I was destined for... wouldn't I? If only the priest had chosen some other commandment to preach about that day, like the one about not coveting your neighbour's oxen, for instance. That I could have coped with.

Although I wouldn't claim that I've been scarred for life by this incident, it's certainly true that I never stole anything ever again, even though I've long since ceased to believe in all the hellfire and brimstone nonsense. Well, okay, there was one teeny-tiny item I "appropriated" a couple of years ago in Greece, but this particular act of thievery could at least be partially justified, and in any case, it was all Penny's fault, Your Honour.

Our toilet cistern had sprung an irreparable leak, so

we'd gone to our nearest DIY superstore (nearly an hour away) and bought a new one of similar size and shape. (I'm not going to name the superstore in question for fear they'll set the police on me after this confession.) It was a bit of a struggle to fit, but I managed it eventually, and all that remained was to connect the flush handle with the flush mechanism inside the cistern. However – and there's always a "however" whenever I undertake any kind of plumbing job – the little piece of angled plastic provided for the purpose didn't seem to fit whichever way I turned and twisted it. Penny had a go, and she was completely baffled as well.

'They had one of these cisterns on display in the shop,' she said. 'Maybe we should go back and see how it's supposed to fit.'

And that's exactly what we did, except when we lifted the lid of the display cistern, the little piece of plastic that connected the flush handle with the flush mechanism was entirely different to the one we'd been supplied with.

'They've obviously given us the wrong part,' said Penny. 'We'll just have to exchange it.'

This would of course have been an excellent idea if not for the fact that I hadn't brought the original fitting with me.

'Why not?' said Penny.

'Well, I thought we were only going to check out how the damn thing connected. It never occurred to me that we'd have to *exchange* it.'

'Perhaps we can just buy it then. It can't be worth more than a few cents.'

'I don't care how much it costs,' I said. 'I'm not paying out for something we should have been given in the first place.'

'Okay, so just put it in your pocket then.'

My mouth dropped open, and the terrifying memory

of the "Grand Theft Tuna Fishing Boat Incident" came flooding back.

'You mean... *steal* it?' I whispered.

'You want to go home and fetch the other one? It's nearly a two hour round trip.'

She had a point, of course, and after some serious soul searching and some more discussion, I finally came to the conclusion that it was the superstore's fault that they'd supplied the wrong part, so what I was about to do could hardly count as stealing. Besides, the next time we were passing, I'd bring back the faulty fitting to fulfil our part of the exchange.

But my conscience wasn't to be so easily fooled, and I could almost smell the sulphurous fumes of Hell as we made our way to the checkout, picking up a pack of clothes pegs on the way so that we didn't arouse suspicion by leaving the store apparently empty-handed.

All of a sudden, I knew exactly how Billy Hayes felt in *Midnight Express* when he's about to go through customs at Istanbul Airport with two kilos of hashish taped to his body: "*I told myself to stay calm. Panic wouldn't help*". But whether he panicked or not, he'd still ended up being sentenced to life imprisonment in a Turkish jail, so despite the ramped-up air conditioning in the shop, the sweat was pouring off me as we waited in line at the checkout. There were only two people in front of us, but everything had gone into slow motion, and by the time it was our turn to be served, my hands were trembling so much that I had to get Penny to hand over the cash for the clothes pegs or I'd have scattered coins in every direction.

The transaction completed, I knew I still couldn't relax until we were back in the car and speeding off up the road, Bonnie and Clyde style. First, we had to run the gauntlet of two uniformed and bored-looking security guards who I was sure were staring at me with deep suspicion. Any second now, they'd step forward and drag me off into a side room where I'd be subjected to a full body search. I could still feel their eyes boring into the back of my skull as we passed and began the long walk through the foyer area to the automatic sliding doors thirty feet away. Thirty feet? It might as well have been thirty miles. As if in one of those terrible nightmares, I was wading through waist-high treacle, making any forward progress almost impossible. Again, I remembered Billy Hayes and how he'd successfully got through customs only to find thirty heavily-armed Turkish soldiers were frisking everyone before allowing them to board the plane.

'I need to use the loo.'

It took me a moment to register what Penny had said, her voice barely audible over the pounding of the blood in my ears.

'You what?' I said, my own voice having somehow risen in pitch by at least two octaves.

'I need to use the loo,' she repeated.

'You can't,' I said. 'Not *here*.'

'Why on earth not?'

'Billy Hayes,' I said. 'Look what happened to Billy Hayes.'

'Billy who?'

'Don't tell me you've never seen *Midnight Express*.'

The blank expression on Penny's face was enough to tell me that she hadn't seen it and that she therefore hadn't the faintest idea of the hell I was going through.

'Look,' I said, lowering my voice to a whispered shriek. 'There's a café a couple of miles up the road. We can stop there and—'

But she was already halfway through the door to the women's toilet, and time again slowed to little more than a crawl while I waited for her to reappear. When she eventually did, I had to stop myself from sprinting out of the exit and across the parking lot to the car. It was only after we'd put a good five miles or so between us and the superstore that I began to calm down, and I gradually reduced the frequency with which I'd been checking the rear-view mirror for a flashing blue light.

Safely back home, it took less than two minutes to fit the ill-gotten piece of plastic inside the toilet cistern, and the satisfying rush of water that followed was almost enough to compensate for the trauma I'd had to endure to achieve it. And I'm sorry, unnamed DIY superstore, but I still haven't been back to return the useless bit of plastic you supplied us with in the first place. Still, I expect you'd only pass it on to some other poor sod who'd waste the best part of an hour trying to figure out how the hell it was supposed to fit, so perhaps I'm doing society a favour.

16

It's a Fair Cop-Out

In hindsight, perhaps I shouldn't have worried quite so much about being placed on the Peloponnese's "Most Wanted" list because although the police in the bigger cities in Greece can be somewhat heavy-handed – particularly when dealing with otherwise peaceful demonstrations – the cops in more rural areas like ours aren't always as assiduous as they might be in the fight against crime. Not that there's much in the way of serious crime around here, although there was an armed robbery in one of the local banks a few years ago when three men with Kalashnikovs got away with about 2,500 euros. It was hardly a major haul considering the risk they'd taken or the potential danger to innocent lives, but perhaps the robbers were aware that the risk of being apprehended wasn't that great in a town like Kyparissia.

The robbery took place at around 2.30 in the afternoon, and the first we saw of any police activity was when two police cars came screaming through the town with lights flashing and sirens blaring at about 7.45 in the evening. According to a Greek friend of ours, 'That's just for show. The police round here don't really want to get caught up in anything where there's guns involved.' And who can blame them?

On another occasion, it was late one night when a member of the public heard a noise outside his flat in the centre of town and looked out of the window to see what was happening. Directly across the street, two men in ski masks were in the process of forcing open the steel shutters of a jeweller's shop, so, as a responsible citizen, he immediately phoned the police.

'I'm sorry, sir,' he was told, 'but the only available officers are too busy elsewhere to attend.'

'Doing what?' asked the man, probably assuming there'd been some horrific triple murder somewhere in the vicinity.

'They're spot-checking car insurance documents at the crossroads a couple of kilometres up the main road.'

This is certainly not as unlikely as it might seem since the cops in Greece are especially conscientious when it comes to motoring offences and even more so when funds are running low at the local constabulary. Fines for even the most basic of road traffic offences can be quite heavy, so a few hours' purge every once in a while is all that's needed to top up the coffers. However, most drivers are aware that such purges are only carried out when the police decide that the weather is pleasant enough to be standing at the side of the road, pointing their speed guns at Lewis Hamilton wannabes. In all the years we've lived in Greece, I've never once seen an officer of the law outdoors in anything so much as the lightest of drizzles.

This is of course good news for the aforementioned Lewis Hamilton wannabes, who seem to believe that road markings and warning signs are merely there for decorative purposes. Many of them appear to have also developed the ability to see round blind bends. I mean, why else would they sit on your rear bumper in their souped-up Toyota hatchback for a couple of kilometres on a perfectly straight road and then decide to overtake just as you're approaching a ninety-degree bend without the slightest possibility of knowing whether there's another vehicle coming towards them on the same side of the road? (The "souping-up", incidentally, is mostly achieved by simply replacing the existing exhaust tailpipe with one that's much bigger, chromier and noisier than the original.) In a country where the way of life is dictated by the mantra *sigá-sigá* (slowly-slowly) in almost every other respect, the act of sitting behind the wheel of a car is apparently sufficient justification to do the exact opposite and drive like a maniac.

The exception, of course, is when someone is driving along a street in town and they realise that the driver of the oncoming car is a friend/colleague/family member. The two vehicles then pull up alongside each other, thereby blocking the whole road, while their occupants carry out a conversation which can sometimes last for several minutes. Meanwhile, the traffic jam continues to build in both directions, but rarely, if ever, is there any murmur of dissent from the drivers who are forced to wait in line until the conversation is concluded. In almost every other country in the world – and certainly in the UK – such a blatant disregard for the free passage of other road users would be met instantly with an ear-splitting cacophony of horn-honking and a tirade of expletive-ridden abuse.

Then there's double-parking, which seems to be perfectly acceptable in Greece as long as you switch on your hazard warning lights. In our nearest town, however, it is still possible to be booked for double-parking even if you have your hazard lights on, although usually only if your registration plate shows that you're not a local. This is because the police are fully aware that any local that they give a ticket to will almost certainly be related to, or a close friend of, another officer in the force or the mayor or some other person with the power to rescind the ticket immediately, so it's hardly worth the bother of writing the ticket in the first place.

And while I'm on the subject of hazard warning lights,

I should point out that their use is extremely popular in Greece and not just for double-parking. In fact, if you're following a vehicle and its hazard lights suddenly come on, it's advisable to keep your distance since this is generally an indication that the driver is about to perform a manoeuvre of some kind and even she/he has no idea what that might be until it's actually carried out – sometimes several kilometres further on up the road. Hazard warning lights are so overused in Greece that imports of replacement bulbs very probably account for at least part of the country's rather alarming trade deficit, so there's an important economic lesson to be learned there, I think.

Another common sight on Greece's highways and byways – and something else that the police turn a blind eye to – is the multi-occupancy moped. This is when an entire family of five or six takes to the open road on a small, two-wheeled machine which has barely enough power to transport much more than a single adult. The struggling moped is often further burdened with several bulging bags of shopping and/or enough cans of olive oil to last the family for the next twelve months.

Failing to exercise proper control of your vehicle is another motoring offence which is largely ignored by the Greek police but would very probably get you a fine and at least a couple of penalty points on your driving licence in the UK. In Greek towns and cities, most people who work in shops or offices don't bother to make their own coffees, etcetera, but order a takeaway instead. This means that they phone their nearest or favourite café (not always the same thing), and the café sends someone on a moped or small motorcycle to deliver their order. The rider therefore has to steer with one hand whilst clutching a drinks-laden tray in the other by means of a tripod arrangement of three connecting wires. I'm always impressed how they very rarely seem to spill so much as a drop as they weave their one-handed way through the traffic and even more impressed that I've never once seen any of them involved in the merest bump of an accident. And how they manage to achieve this when it's raining and they're also holding an umbrella is a total mystery.

Not all Greek drivers are maniacs with scant regard for road safety, of course, any more than British drivers are all to-the-letter devotees of the rules and principles of the Highway Code, and experience has taught me that driving in Greece is infinitely preferable to driving in Italy. Rush hour in the centre of Florence and an abandoned attempt to get back on the motorway outside Milan are just two of the instances that I wouldn't want to repeat in a hurry – or even very slowly. Penny and I have driven between Greece and the UK several times since we moved here, and we always breathe a sigh of relief when we've managed to get through Italy with body and vehicle still miraculously intact.

On one of these trips back to the UK, we had an overnight stop in Italy at a small hotel near to Lake Como, but the narrow streets made it impossible to park anywhere near.

'How about parking?' I asked the manager when we checked in.

'Not a problem,' he said. 'The hotel has its own underground garage a few minutes' walk from here.'

'Okay, so how do I get there?'

'It's not easy to explain,' he said with a knowing smile that suggested he'd somehow deduced my almost complete inability to follow even the simplest of directions just by looking at me. 'I'll have to come with you and show you the way.'

So, once we'd offloaded our bags and leaving Penny behind, the hotel manager climbed into the passenger seat of our car and told me to drive to the roundabout at the end of the road. Inevitably, it was right in the middle of rush hour by now, and when we got to the roundabout I waited patiently for a gap in the hurtling stream of vehicles coming at me from my left.

'I can tell you're British,' said the manager after a couple of stationary minutes.

'Oh?' I said. 'Why's that then?'

'Because we'll be stuck here all night if you carry on sitting here like this. You have to push in.'

'Push in?' The guy was quite right. The very idea was totally at odds with my deeply entrenched and characteristically British sense of "waiting one's turn".

'You just have to go for it. They'll let you in, I promise.'

Not at all convinced, I stayed put for another thirty seconds or so and then shot forward in front of a car which I considered to be the least likely to cause too much damage in case of a collision – a Fiat 500.

Thankfully, the Fiat driver did appear to ease off the throttle by a fraction of a kilometre per hour, and the anticipated crunch of metal against metal was narrowly averted.

'You see?' said the manager, and I knew without looking that he was wearing a grin so smug it would have made the Cheshire Cat look like a manic depressive with heartburn.

After that, all went relatively smoothly, although I have to admit that the hotel manager had also been right about not being able to find the underground garage on my own. The mind-boggling labyrinth of narrow, one-way streets would have made even the most directionally gifted give up in despair, and I am very definitely not in that league. Even with my expert local guide, it took us the best part of twenty minutes to reach the garage and park up, but less than five to walk back to the hotel.

Needless to say, however, I got hopelessly lost the

following morning when I set off to pick up the car and wished we'd stopped off in Switzerland instead of Italy. At least in Switzerland there would have been far more likelihood of coming across a passing Saint Bernard with a stress-busting barrel of brandy and an unfailing ability to lead me safely back to civilisation.

17

Lost in Translation

One of our earliest bad experiences of driving in Greece was nobody's fault but our own, and we weren't even moving at the time. "The Thoroughly Annoying Incident of Locking Ourselves Out of the Camper Van" was one of those nightmare situations when at the very moment you begin the action of slamming the door, you notice that the keys are still in the ignition. Everything goes into slow motion, but you're in slow motion as well, so there's no way you're going to react quickly enough to stop the door from closing before it's too late. Inevitably, the bag containing all our essential items such as passports, driving licences, bank cards and, of course, the spare van key were still inside the van.

My youth had not been so misspent as to have acquired the necessary expertise for *subtly* breaking into cars, so there was nothing for it but to smash one of the windows. On the basis that the smallest window would be the least expensive to replace, I set about the offside quarterlight with a conveniently nearby rock. (I'm not sure if vehicles still have quarterlights these days, so for anyone too young to remember them, a quarterlight is a small triangular window which is usually hinged and used for ventilation.) But however hard I whacked the glass, the rock just bounced off and inflicted little more than the faintest of scratches.

Time for Plan B, which was to walk the mile or so

into town and find the nearest garage. Surely they'd have a whole range of fancy, sophisticated gadgets for getting into a locked vehicle with minimal effort and without inflicting any damage at all.

Communicating our problem to the mechanic presented a major challenge since he didn't speak a word of English and our knowledge of Greek was still at the "Hello, my name is Rob. What is your name?" stage. So, apart from establishing that the mechanic's name was Grigoris, we didn't get very far with Plan B until we resorted to an elaborate and rather complicated mime which even Marcel Marceau would have been hard put to have found fault with.

And so at last we climbed into Grigoris's pickup, and we (Penny actually) directed him to our van with a series of hand gestures. As soon as we got there, Grigoris circumnavigated the entire van and tried every single door and window, presumably because he thought that if we were stupid enough to lock ourselves out in the first place, we were probably stupid enough not to have checked them ourselves.

'Now we'll see how the experts do it,' I said to Penny, expecting the mechanic to pull out of his toolbox a handy little gadget designed for the express purpose of unlocking a car door.

Instead, he produced a heavy-duty lump hammer and handed it to me with a series of gestures which appeared to indicate that I should smash one of the windows with it. In response to a gesture of my own that I intended to convey "Why me? You're the bloody expert", Grigoris made a big show of rubbing his lower back and grimacing with pain.

'Oh, you've got a bad back, have you?' I said.

Grigoris clearly didn't understand – or pretended not to – so he simply shrugged, tapped at the quarterlight on the passenger side of the van and took a few steps backwards.

Not having much choice in the matter, I took an admittedly tentative swing at the glass with the lump hammer, which, not unlike the rock earlier, almost bounced out of my hand with the recoil. Grigoris gave me a "You'll have to give it a lot more welly than that" kind of look, so I did – several times. Eventually, the hammer put a big enough crack in the glass for Grigoris to remove it completely with the triumphant flourish of a master of his craft. Yes, I did all the work, and he took all the glory, which didn't bother me in the slightest, especially when he told us he wouldn't accept any payment for his help.

The next job was to get a replacement pane for the quarterlight, but this was apparently beyond Grigoris's remit, so we checked out the other local garages until we found one with a VW sign outside. It was as good a place as any to start, but before going in, we checked our English-Greek dictionary for the appropriate vocabulary. This was when we had our first encounter with one of the many difficulties involved in attempting to master the Greek language. There are many examples in Greek where two words are spelt exactly the same but mean something entirely different, depending on which syllable is stressed. This can lead to some highly embarrassing – and sometimes downright dangerous – situations if you happen to put the stress in the wrong place. More on that later, but on this occasion, we discovered that the word for window pane is *tzámι* and the word for mosque is *tzamí*. (In case you missed the bit at the beginning of this book where I've added a few notes about the conventions I've followed for Greek words, I'll just repeat that a little mark over a vowel tells you which syllable to stress. So, *tzámι* is pronounced TZA-mee and *tzamí* is pronounced tza-MEE.)

Not surprisingly, we took our time practising the

correct pronunciation before venturing into the garage so we'd avoid a conversation along the lines of:

US: Excuse me, but we'd like a replacement mosque for our camper van.

MECHANIC: I'm sorry, we don't do part exchange.

US: No, you don't understand. We don't want to *sell* the van. We just need a small, triangular mosque for it.

MECHANIC: You want a small mosque for *inside* the van? Triangular?

US: We broke the last one unfortunately.

MECHANIC: You broke a *mosque*?

US: Smashed hell out of it with a lump hammer, yes. We didn't really have much choice.

(The mechanic lets out a low whistle, as only a mechanic can, takes off his baseball cap and scratches his head.)

MECHANIC: You do realise that people have had a fatwa put out on them for a lot less than that?

US: For breaking a mosque?

MECHANIC: Are you serious? It makes Salman Rushdie seem like the Ayatollah's best mate.

It would have been at about this point that the mechanic would have told us that he didn't want anything more to do with us and to take our blasphemous business elsewhere. Then he would have turned his back and buried his head inside the engine compartment of whatever vehicle he happened to be working on at the time.

Fortunately, however, our exaggerated pronunciation of *tzámı* seemed to avoid any such misunderstanding because the very next day, Stathis the mechanic rang us to say the replacement glass had arrived (by bus from Athens) and that we should bring the van in so he could fit it.

This was our first experience of the "*tzámı-tzamí*" type of trap for the linguistically unwary, but there were many more to follow. Take the time, for instance, when local father and son farmer duo, Thanassis and Yiorgos, came to help us set up an irrigation system for some of our olive trees. We were halfway through the job of laying a network of plastic pipes which led from a pump at the well, when Penny and I remembered that we had an appointment in town on some official business or other. It wasn't something we could get out of, so we apologised to Thanassis and Yiorgos for leaving them in the lurch and asked if we could get anything for them while we were out.

Their only request was for two soft, white loaves, which should have been perfectly easy except for one thing. The Greek word for "soft" is *malaká*, which happens to be remarkably similar to the word *maláka*, and that means something entirely different and not at all polite. The closest equivalent in English is probably "tosser", and it's a word that you'll hear frequently in Greece, either as a kind of playful endearment or as a gross insult, depending on how it's delivered. Consequently, and as in the case of the "*tzámı-tzamí*" incident at the garage, we rehearsed the appropriate pronunciation until we were absolutely certain that we weren't going to walk into the bakery and say, 'Two white loaves, please, you tosser' and end up with our arses kicked – or worse.

Other words which can cause confusion and can potentially lead to an embarrassing situation, although not necessarily result in the unwary speaker suffering physical violence, are as follows:

Kounávi (pine marten) and *kouniáda* (sister-in-law). Although these two Greek words don't look as similar to each other as, for instance, *tzámi* and *tzamí*, I did once misunderstand a farmer friend who I thought was telling me that their pine marten had just died. I expressed my condolences, of course, but was somewhat surprised that a farmer of all people would keep a pine marten as a pet, never mind be quite so upset about its demise. Given that pine martens have a reputation for decimating entire flocks of sheep and chickens, most Greek farmers don't think twice before shooting them on sight. On the other side of the coin, it's always advisable to ask someone to repeat what they've said if you believe they've just confessed to shooting their sister-in-law.

Syllypitíria (commiserations) and *syncharitíria* (congratulations). While I'm on the subject of commiserating, and although these two Greek words don't look particularly similar either, I can never remember which is which, so I usually refrain from using them at all. Commiserating with someone who's just told you that they'd won the lottery only makes you look stupid unless you're known to be some kind of fundamentalist with very strong views about the burden of personal wealth. On the other hand, congratulating someone because their house has been burned to the ground would be infinitely worse.

Pípa (pipe for smoking) and *pípa* (er...). The thing is, these two words are exactly the same and pronounced in exactly the same way, but whereas the first meaning is perfectly innocuous (unless you happen to be an anti-smoking zealot), the second is... well, a tad risqué. If you're easily offended, don't read the rest of this sentence, but for everyone else, *pípa* is also a slang word for fellatio. The reason I know this, I hasten to add, is because a Greek friend phoned me during the wedding of Prince William and Kate Middleton. Not an obvious connection, I know, but bear with me a moment and I'll explain.

'Are you watching the Royal Wedding on TV?' Petros asked, barely able to contain his laughter.

'No.'

'Well, turn it on.'

'Which channel?'

'Doesn't matter. Nearly all the Greek stations are showing it.'

I did as I was told but – apart from some of the wedding guests' hats – I didn't see what he found so hysterically funny.

'It's Kate Middleton's sister,' said Petros. 'Every so often, the cameras focus in on her arse, and the commentators almost piss themselves laughing when they mention her name.'

He let out his own guffaw of laughter but stopped immediately when I told him I had no idea what Kate Middleton's sister's name was other than Ms Middleton.

'You don't *know*?' He seemed utterly astonished that, as a Brit, I was unable to name the sibling of the soon-to-be-wife of the second in line to the throne.

'It's Pippa,' he said with obvious glee, 'but all the commentators keep pronouncing it as "peepa".'

'Oh, I see.'

Petros could tell that I still hadn't got the joke, and that's when I came to learn that sometimes a *pípa* is not just a pipe.

Domáta (tomato) and ***domátio*** (room). To restore the tone a little, these two Greek words are very similar and can lead to a variety of awkward misunderstandings, particularly when trying to book a hotel room, for instance. Not only that, but if you were to combine this with some of the other examples above (tactfully avoiding *pípa*), you could quite easily find yourself phoning a hotel and asking for "a double tomato for my wife and I, preferably with a mosque overlooking the sea, and a separate tomato for my pine marten". And if you were keen to have a nice, soft bed, you might also finish with "and I'd like mattresses in both tomatoes, you tosser".

Somehow I think you'd be told that the hotel was booked solid for the next several months.

18

A Ferret's Toe

When Penny and I first made the decision to move to Greece, one of her aunts, who'd travelled extensively in her lifetime, gave us an excellent piece of advice.

'Whenever you visit a foreign country,' she said, 'always make sure that the first word you learn in their language is the word for "wonderful".'

She explained that even if it was the *only* word you knew, it could come in handy in a whole variety of situations. If, for instance, someone invited you for a meal, you could point at the food and say "wonderful", or if someone asked you what you thought of their country – "wonderful". The weather? The architecture? The beach? The beer? The price of fish? All "wonderful". Even if the food made you want to gag, the weather was atrocious, all the buildings looked like they'd been designed by a crack-addicted baboon, the beaches were filthy, the beer tasted like pee-flavoured vinegar, and half a dozen sardines would cost you the best part of a day's pay, the magic word "wonderful" would invariably elicit the same response – a proudly beaming smile and a friend for life.

The word for "wonderful" in Greek, incidentally, is *thavmásios*, but Penny and I had linguistic ambitions far beyond such a limited vocabulary. So, armed with a small fortune's worth of CDs and books, we set about the task of learning Greek with the dangerously naive enthusiasm of an insect that's just caught a whiff of the nectar from a Venus Fly Trap.

I've always been interested in language and, although I say so myself, seem to have had quite a knack for learning foreign languages both ancient and modern, from Old Norse and Anglo Saxon to French and German. However, it had been many years since I'd flexed my brain's language-learning muscles, and I very quickly discovered that age is no friend to the aspiring polyglot. Not only that, but as soon as I opened our copy of *Fluent Greek in Twenty Minutes* and scanned the first page, I realised that of all the twenty-four letters in the Greek alphabet, I was familiar with about three.

'Listen to this recording of a conversation between Maria and Kostas and follow the transcript in the book,' said the soothingly calm voice of the woman on the CD.

Follow the transcript? Are you serious? It was going to take me days just to decipher the first sentence. Now I knew how Alan Turing felt when he took his first look at the Enigma Code.

'It's really not that difficult,' said Penny, rather smugly in my opinion. 'After all, there's two less letters than there are in the English alphabet.'

'It's all right for you,' I said. 'You did all that sciencey stuff at school, so you know most of the Greek letters already. I told you we should have moved to Spain. At least they have the same bloody alphabet as us. Even Latin has the same alphabet as us.'

'That's because the English alphabet *is* the Latin alphabet.'

I knew that already, of course, so I simply grunted a "whatever" and carried on with the uphill struggle of trying to understand what the hell Maria and Kostas were banging on about. Were they really planning a terrorist attack on their local greengrocer's shop or were they merely trying to decide whether to have beer or wine with their meal?

One of the better book/CD combinations we used was published by the BBC. I mean, you can't go wrong with the ever-reliable BBC, can you? Well, yes, actually you can. There were at least two fairly major errors that we only discovered to be errors when we moved to Greece and began to put our hard-won linguistic knowledge into practice. The first, and perhaps slightly less important of the two, was the pronunciation of *sigá-sigá*, which, like *maláka*, is an expression that you'll hear quite often in Greece and translates literally as "slowly-slowly". According to the BBC, it's pronounced *síga-síga* (as in seeker-seeker), but as we soon found out after hearing the expression several times within just a few hours of our arrival in Greece, the correct pronunciation is *sigá-sigá* (as in cigar-cigar), with the stress on the second syllable and not the first. As far as I'm aware, the BBC's version – *síga-síga* – doesn't mean anything at all in Greek, so at least we wouldn't have been in the *maláka/malaká* type of situation and unintentionally told someone that their grandfather was the illegitimate son of a hippopotamus or somesuch. And in any case, we're British, so there was very little likelihood that we'd ever have cause to use an expression like *sigá-sigá* since we're genetically and culturally programmed to strike while the iron's hot, shake a leg and generally get a move on.

Even so, we were shocked and dismayed at the misinformation we'd been fed by that mighty bastion of reliability, the British Broadcasting Corporation. But little did we know that worse was yet to come.

On the first three occasions that we ate out in Greece – at three different tavernas – we felt a glowing sense of pride in being able to order our food in almost fluent Greek. "Almost" because the BBC had made a crucially important mistake in every one of the many "eating out in Greece" examples on its CD. Please note, Director General of the BBC, if you happen to be reading this, the Greek word for chips is *not* and never has been *tiganités*. It's not even a noun. It's an adjective, and it just means "fried".

Little wonder then that each time we ordered *tiganités*, the waiter stared blankly at us, his or her pen poised over their notepad as they waited patiently – and ultimately forlornly – for a recognisable noun. Thinking that we'd perhaps pronounced the word incorrectly, we'd repeat it a few more times with a variety of inflections but always with the same result.

'It's no good simply repeating "fried" over and over again with slight variations in inflection,' the waiter was probably thinking. 'Just tell me exactly *what* you want fried so we can all get on with our lives before it's too late and we all die of starvation.'

As we later learned, the Greek word for chips is *patátes*, and although you might be thinking that ordering "potatoes" is also rather vague, it is a truth universally acknowledged – or at least in Greece – that what you're asking for is a plate of chips. Not potatoes roasted in the oven with lemon, or mashed potatoes mixed with ridiculous amounts of garlic, but chips. If you want your potatoes in any other form than chips, then you make it perfectly clear when you place your order, and as a brief but relevant aside, if you ask for "chips" (*tsips*) in Greece, you'll be given a packet of crisps – more than likely oregano-flavoured.

Still on the subject of learning Greek from book/CD packages, it will hardly surprise you to know that the one I mentioned earlier called *Fluent Greek in Twenty Minutes* doesn't actually exist. One that does exist and makes not unreasonable but still exaggerated claims is *Learn Greek in Three Months*. The reason I know this is not only because we used it ourselves, but because

Penny's mum did as well. This came as quite a shock to us when she brandished her library-borrowed copy at us the moment we walked through her front door less than a week after we'd made our announcement about moving to Greece.

'I've started learning Greek, darlings,' she beamed, which instantly rang alarm bells.

Penny and I exchanged horrified glances, and an unspoken thought passed between us: "Oh God, she doesn't think she's coming too, does she?"

Granny – everyone calls her Granny – must have read our minds because she quickly added, 'Don't worry, dears. I'm not planning to come with you, but I'm sure I'll be visiting fairly often, and I thought it would be rather fun to learn some of the language.'

Yes, Granny does use words like "darlings" and "dears" and sounds not unlike the Queen, which is quite odd really because she was born and brought up in the East End of London. Born within the sound of Bow Bells, in fact, so yer actual proper Cockney until she went to a posh school in Cheltenham where dropped H's and glottal stops were not to be tolerated. The result is that she now says things like 'I'm going to take a shah [shower]' and 'I need to arn [iron] some clothes'. Particularly ironic was when she played the part of a Cockney maid in an amateur dramatic society's production of *An Inspector Calls* but was apparently unable – or unwilling – to resurrect her original accent. The bizarre result sounded like an even posher version of Maggie Smith's Dowager Countess of Grantham in *Downton Abbey* delivering lines such as "Cor blamee, guvnah, but Ay've been up and darn them epples and pears all deh lake a brade's natie and no misteck".

Hearing Granny's early – and continuing to this day – attempts at speaking Greek with the self-same upper-class accent is a source of equal amusement, and that first evening was no exception. As we sat down to eat, she began to impress/amuse us by reeling off the handful of Greek words she'd learned so far.

'That's very impressive,' said Penny, stifling a giggle. 'You're doing nearly as well as us.'

'Well, darling, I have a technique for learning vocabulary, you see. Every time I try to learn a new word, I think of a visual image to go with it, which makes it a lot easier to remember. The Greek word for "thank you", for instance, is *efcharistó*, which sounds rather like "a ferret's toe", so that's what I picture in my mind when I want to remember the word. And if I wanted to say "thank you very much", I'd think of a parrot called Polly as well.'

'As in *efcharistó pára polí?*' said Penny.

'That's right.'

'So whenever you want to thank someone in Greek, you first have to imagine a ferret's toe?' I said.

'Precisely.'

'But surely that requires a pretty detailed knowledge of what a whole range of small mammals' feet look like. I mean, you don't want to end up thanking somebody by saying "a weasel's toe", do you?'

Granny gave me one of her famous blank looks, which clearly conveyed that she had no idea whether I was joking or not. As is the norm in such cases, she considered the possibility for a few brief seconds, then decided to ignore the remark altogether and carried on with her original train of thought.

'There *is* one Greek word that really stumps me, though,' she said, 'and for the life of me I just *cannot* think of an image to go with it.'

'Oh?' said Penny. 'What word is that?'

'It's the word for "miss", as in "mister" and "missus".'

Neither Penny nor I had come across it in our own

134

language studies so far, and to be honest, neither of us thought it was likely to feature in anybody's list of "Essential Greek Vocabulary for Beginners". Anybody except Granny, that is.

'We don't know it either,' I said. 'So what is it?'

Granny then flicked to the glossary at the back of *Learn Greek in Three Months*, located the word and read it aloud. '"This penis".'

Our mouths dropped open in disbelief as Penny and I struggled to convince ourselves that she really had just said "this penis", and this was immediately followed by a tsunami of hysterical laughter from the pair of us.

'So you've got this word "this penis",' I said, wiping away a tear when I had sufficiently recovered the power of speech, 'and you can't think of a single visual image to go with it?'

'Not a single one, darling. I don't suppose either of you can think of anything, can you?'

(In the interests of accuracy, the word she was trying to remember was *thespinés*, and the correct pronunciation is "thespeeness" with the stress on the last syllable.)

Granny's extraordinary naivety is almost legendary, and especially – as should be quite obvious by now – where matters of a sexual nature are concerned. How she ever managed to produce five children is a total mystery to everyone who knows her, including her five children.

As a footnote to Granny and the "this penis" story, we reminded her of it during one of her annual five-week visits here a couple of years later, and she remembered it well, adding, 'Yes, darlings. "This penis". You know, I never could get my tongue round it.'

Enough said, I think.

19

Inkwells and Quivers

Despite all of our efforts to master as much of the language as possible even before we moved to Greece, we still struggled to make ourselves understood or understand what people were saying to us. In the first week or so, we even had trouble mastering what you might expect to be the simplest two words in almost any language – the words for "yes" and "no". In Greek they seem totally counterintuitive, since *nai* means "yes" and *óchi* means "no", and I'm sure we can't be the only native English speakers who think that *nai* sounds like "no" and *óchi* sounds like "okay". We could therefore probably be forgiven for sometimes getting them the wrong way round (occasionally with embarrassing and/or unwanted consequences).

Something else we had to get used to very quickly was the *non-verbal* version of "no". This involves a slight backward tilt of the head and, for extra emphasis, is often accompanied by a click of the tongue, which sounds not unlike a "tut". And if you really want to drive the point home, you can also add a sideways wag of the index finger. The first few times we were confronted with this reaction to what we believed to be our perfectly reasonable questions, we were somewhat taken aback by such a seemingly brusque response. To us, the combined effect of the head tilt, the tutting and the finger wagging came across as the non-verbal equivalent of "Of course not. Are you stupid or what?", but we soon learned that this was an entirely normal and acceptable way to just say "no". On the other hand, "Are you stupid or what?" might well have been meant literally when a friend of ours got her Greek words mixed up in a local mini-market and asked if they sold donkeys when she'd meant to ask for gloves.

Since the area where we live is largely agricultural, it's not a big surprise that very few people speak English. There's no reason why they should, of course, and unlike plenty of Brits abroad, we don't expect every other person in the world to have at least a basic knowledge of English.

Consequently, when we first arrived in Greece, we never went anywhere without our pocket English-Greek dictionary and phrasebook, although we soon discovered that the latter was entirely inappropriate for most of our needs. Given that we'd bought a five-acre farm with four hundred and twenty olive trees, seventy grapevines and a whole variety of fruit and nut trees, the standard phrasebook sections of "At the Hotel", "At the Restaurant", "At the Railway Station" and so on were of little or no help at all. What we really could have done with was some kind of specialist phrasebook with sections like "At the Agricultural Supplies Shop", "At the Ministry of Agriculture Office" and "At the Chainsaw Repair Shop". I vowed at the time that one day, when my Greek was good enough, I would produce such a handy little booklet myself. Thirteen years later and I haven't even started it and probably never will, partly because my Greek still isn't good enough but mostly because I imagine the market for such a publication is minute if not non-existent.

And while I'm on the subject of phrasebooks, we were particularly intrigued with one that a friend brought with her when she came for a visit. Unusually, as well as the standard hotel/restaurant/railway station stuff, this phrasebook had an entire section devoted to "Romance and Dating". This was divided into sub-sections and began fairly innocuously with "At the Disco" and "At the Beach Bar" and included pretty lame chat-up lines of the "Do you come here often?" variety. Towards the end of the "Romance and Dating" section, however, the "useful phrases" got steadily and decidedly raunchier, and the final sub-section, "In the Bedroom", even had the Greek translation of "Please untie me now". A rather bizarre inclusion in itself, but since the person wanting to use this phrase presumably had their hands tied, I wonder quite how they were supposed to pick up the phrasebook and turn to the right page in order to say *"Parakaló lýse me tóra"*.

Anyway, to return to the real world of ordering organic fertiliser and ecologically sound traps for olive pests in Greek, it quickly became clear to us that we were in desperate need of more help with our language learning than was to be found in any amount of books and CDs. The urgency for this was finally and rather alarmingly brought home to us – and particularly me – after a brief "conversation" I'd had with Pavlos, the local tractor repair man. By this time, I'd developed the rather bad habit of pretending to understand almost everything that was said to me in Greek even though I barely understood more than one word in ten. I've absolutely no idea why I did this unless it was for some subconscious notion that it would be impolite *not* to understand, but whatever the reason, I'd nod sagely and throw in the odd word I *did* know like *nai* (yes) and *entáxei* (okay) and even *katalavaíno* (I understand) while someone rattled on incomprehensibly at us in Greek.

The first time this happened, Penny was clearly impressed that I'd seemed to understand everything that had been said.

'What were they saying?' she asked when the conversation ended and we were on our own again.

'I haven't got a clue,' I admitted.

'So why did you pretend you understood?'

'I really don't know. It just seemed like the right thing to do at the time.'

Penny then pointed out that this wasn't very sensible since I could possibly have been agreeing to all kinds of things that we really wouldn't want to agree to. I knew she was right, of course, but it didn't stop me repeating the same sort of charade on several subsequent occasions. The only difference now was that Penny would wander off after my first couple of nods and an *entáxei* and leave me to it. And that's exactly what she did seconds after Pavlos collared us in the local supermarket.

It was quite a lengthy – if very one-sided – conversation, and from the odd few words I was able to pick up, it was something about a tractor. (Admittedly, this wasn't especially difficult since the Greek word for tractor is *traktér*.) When we'd first visited Xerika with a view to buying the place, we'd seen a very old tractor and various attachments on the land and had agreed to buy them on top of what we paid for the property. However, that winter (2003/2004) was the harshest the country had seen in over thirty years, and since nobody bothered much with anti-freeze, the tractor's engine block had cracked, so it was virtually a write-off. Fortunately, we hadn't handed over any money for it yet, and Pavlos had come and towed it down to his yard to keep it for spare parts.

This was about two years before we bumped into him in the supermarket, and apart from the word *traktér*, I had very little idea what he was going on about. So, when I eventually caught up with Penny and she inevitably asked me what Pavlos had been saying, I pulled a sheepish face and admitted the usual truth.

'Although,' I added even more sheepishly, 'and you have to promise not to get angry, but there's ever such a slight possibility that he was asking if we wanted to buy our old tractor back.'

'Oh God, please don't tell me you stood there nodding and saying *nai* and *entáxei* like you usually do.'

Well, I couldn't deny it, and it didn't do a lot to sweeten the pill when I mumbled, 'Um, it's also possible that two thousand euros might have been mentioned.'

This is genuinely what I believed had been the gist of what Pavlos had said to me, and for the next two weeks or so, I winced visibly every time I heard any kind of vehicle coming up our track. Mercifully, though, Pavlos never did show up with our old tractor, but I'd certainly learnt my lesson, and from that day to this, I haven't once pretended to understand when I didn't.

As I said earlier, it was this potentially disastrous incident with Pavlos which ultimately convinced us that we were in urgent need of some additional help in our desperate battle to get to grips with the Greek language. And as chance would have it, it was at about this time that the local authority was starting a series of Greek lessons in the town, and since the lessons were funded by the European Union and therefore free, we signed up immediately. The only real drawback was that the course began in exactly the same week as our olive harvest started. This meant that by the time we'd finished harvesting for the day, we were already utterly exhausted, and after grabbing a quick shower, we were at our desks in the local school at six in the evening. Needless to say, we were hardly at our most receptive for a twice-weekly two-hour session of intensive language learning.

If we hadn't been quite so desperate to improve our Greek, we probably wouldn't have bothered at all, and after the very first lesson, we came even closer to abandoning the course altogether.

'I don't know about learning Greek,' I said to Penny as we left the classroom, 'but we've just been treated to the perfect lesson in how *not* to teach a foreign language.'

Now, I'm well aware that this sounds incredibly arrogant of me, but in my defence, I am a qualified teacher of English as a foreign language, so I believe I do know what I'm talking about. Throughout my TESOL (Teaching English to Speakers of Other Languages) course, one of the cardinal rules that was drummed into us repeatedly was that you should never teach for more than forty-five minutes at a time without giving your students – and yourself – a short break. But we'd just endured a solid two hours without so much as a hastily taken "comfort break", as it's rather quaintly called nowadays, so little or nothing had sunk in during the last hour and a quarter.

Not that we'd learned that much in the first forty-five minutes either, to be honest, and as a final nail in the coffin of the lesson as a whole, the teacher sent us on our way with a page of vocabulary she'd typed up which we had to learn before the next lesson. Bearing in mind that this was a beginners' class supposedly aimed at learning Greek for everyday purposes, several of the thirty-or-so words on the list seemed totally inappropriate. "Inkwell", for example. Do they even exist outside museums any more? And what about "quiver"? Not the verb meaning "tremble" but the noun meaning the container you put your arrows in. I really can't imagine many occasions when you'd need to use either "inkwell" or "quiver" in general conversation unless you happen to have discovered the secret of travelling back in time, but apparently our teacher thought they deserved to be included in the first thirty words that all Greek language beginners should know.

So disappointing was our first lesson that it might also have been our last, but we decided to persevere, and I'm actually glad that we did. On the positive side, there were only Penny and I and another English couple in the class, and even they dropped out after the first two weeks. This meant that Penny and I had the teacher's full and undivided attention, and as we got to know her better, we could even persuade her to gear the lessons to our particular needs. On occasions, she also acted as our translator when we took in some official Greek form that we had to complete. And in all fairness, her methods improved dramatically after that first lesson in how not to teach a foreign language. Perhaps she'd been nervous or intimidated by us, and maybe she'd been in too much of a hurry when she'd cobbled together the vocabulary list, but never again did we hear the words *melanodocheio* (inkwell) or *farétra* (quiver).

After about six months, however, the lessons came to an abrupt end when our heavily pregnant teacher announced that she was going on maternity leave, so once again, Penny and I were left to our own language-learning devices. That was more than ten years ago, and since then, Penny has been far more self-motivated than I have and even reads novels in Greek with the English version alongside as backup. It's a matter of great embarrassment to me – shame almost – that after all these years, my knowledge of Greek should be a hell of a lot better than it is. It's not that I'm particularly lazy or that I don't *want* to learn. It's more that I came to the conclusion a long time ago that however hard I worked at it and for however many years, I'd never be able to speak Greek to the level I aspired to. It may seem absurd, but I developed an attitude of "If I'll never be able to speak Greek like a native, then what's the point in trying?" Absurd, as I say, but it's an acknowledged character flaw of mine that I seem to have been stuck with for most of my life. Even as a kid, for instance, I gave up learning to play the guitar because I couldn't play like Jimi Hendrix or Eric Clapton after only a couple of weeks of lessons.

I haven't given up completely on trying to learn Greek. Not at all, but I certainly don't put in anything like the effort that Penny does, and the difference shows. Having said that, it's become quite clear to us that Penny is much better at understanding Greek than I am, whereas I probably speak it rather better than she does. Perhaps this indicates something about our personalities – that Penny's a much better listener than I am (she is a psychological therapist after all), and I'm just gobby. Or is that simply a difference between men and women generally?

One of the things that I think has really hampered us in our attempts to learn Greek is that where we live is very isolated. Our nearest neighbour is about two kilometres away, so we rarely get the opportunity to practise our Greek as we would on an almost daily basis if we lived in a village or town. In our early days in Greece, we tried to compensate for this by setting aside at least an hour each day when Penny and I would communicate exclusively in Greek, but it was a strategy that was very short-lived. After all, there's a limit to the number of times you can have the same inane conversation in any language:

'Would you like a cup of tea?'
'Yes, please. I would like a cup of tea very much.'
'Would you like milk with your tea?'
'Yes, please. I would like milk with my tea.'
'Would you like sugar with your tea?'
'Yes, please. I would like one sugar with my tea.'

Not only was the daily repetition of this kind of "conversation" of minimal benefit in improving our

Greek, but it was pointlessly artificial as well. And if I couldn't remember from one day to the next whether Penny took milk and/or sugar in her tea, then I'd be seriously concerned about the state of my mental health.

20

The Forth Road Bridge Disaster

I've mentioned in previous chapters the importance of correct pronunciation when attempting to speak Greek as well as the potential dangers of mispronouncing various words. Believe it or not, and even though my knowledge of Greek vocabulary and grammar is still at the C-minus stage, I have sometimes been complimented on my accent. This, I am sure, is because in our early days of living in Greece, I hit upon the notion that every time I said anything in Greek, I should adopt a kind of Native American accent heard in many of the older "Cowboys 'n' Injuns" films. Something along the lines of Tonto's "White man speak with forked tongue" way of speaking in *The Lone Ranger*. (Incidentally, I'm referring here to the TV series from many years ago, and as I haven't seen the 2013 movie version, I don't know if this is how Johnny Depp speaks.) It seemed to work quite well the first few times I tried it, so it's a technique I've used ever since.

To give a brief example, it was a few years ago when some of the family came to visit us and we'd gone for a drink at one of the local beach bars. The waiter arrived at our table and asked each one of us what we wanted to order. When it got to Penny's daughter's turn, she asked for a Sprite, but the waiter responded with an expression of blank incomprehension, so Naomi repeated it.

'Sprite, please.'

Another blank look and another repetition before I stepped in with my best Tonto impression and said, 'Spraït.'

The waiter's face lit up. 'Ah, *Spraït*,' he said, seemingly delighted that there was at least one person in our group who could actually speak his language.

I've been to France enough times in my life to know for certain that, if you're British, waiters – especially in the cities and larger towns – often pretend that they don't understand a word you're on about, however good your French might be. But this isn't true of the Greeks at all. Slightly patronising though it might sound, they really do appreciate it when foreigners have taken the trouble to learn even a handful of Greek words and phrases, but they sometimes struggle to understand if your pronunciation is a little wayward.

A Greek friend suggested a reason for this once, which seems perfectly plausible, and it's because there are very few variations in accent throughout the whole of Greece, so Greek people have very little experience of having to interpret a different pronunciation from their own. Conversely, the Brits are totally accustomed to understanding a whole range of accents, which vary quite dramatically over such a relatively small geographical area.

As someone who was born and brought up in the south of England, however, I must admit that I was utterly baffled by the Geordie accent on my first visit to Newcastle. I'd only just arrived and needed petrol for the car, so I pulled into a garage and filled up. No problem there, but then I went into the shop to pay. This was before the days of debit and credit cards, and I stood at the counter with my open chequebook and asked who I should make the cheque payable to. The attendant said something in what might as well have been Klingon, so I asked again and got the same response. After the third time of asking and completely unable to understand the reply, the situation was becoming more than a little embarrassing. I still had the pen in my hand and a blank cheque in front of me, so it was hardly one of those occasions where I could simply smile and nod and then walk away. Finally, in desperation, the attendant rummaged under the counter and retrieved a letterhead with the garage's name printed at the top and angrily slammed it on the counter.

'Ah, I see,' I said, writing out the cheque and wondering since when "Chertreeserstay" was supposed to mean "Cherry Tree Service Station".

Besides having to be careful with your pronunciation in Greece, you also need to be wary of using slang or idioms when talking to an English-speaking Greek, regardless of how fluent they might be. Since I'd previously taught English as a foreign language, this was something that wasn't at all new to me. Penny, on the other hand, had had no such background, and I often found myself having to "translate" some of her more obscure words and phrases such as "We got ourselves into a right pickle", "Bob's your uncle", "That's a different kettle of fish altogether" and "It all went a bit pear-shaped". She wasn't entirely happy about my frequently correcting her, but she did get her revenge one day when I inadvertently used an expression that plenty of native English speakers probably wouldn't even know.

The gaffe happened when we were talking to a guy called Dionysis, who runs our local olive press. We'd been telling him that we were just about to go back to the UK for a week or two and we were desperately trying to get everything sorted out on the land before we left.

'One of the biggest jobs is getting all the grass cut,' I said.

'Yes,' said Dionysis, 'and at this time of year, it keeps

growing back again as soon as you've cut it.'

'Exactly,' I said. 'So with twenty *strémma* [20,000 square metres/5 acres], you have to start all over again as soon as you've finished. It's like painting the Forth Road Bridge.'

I knew it was a mistake the moment the words were out of my mouth, and Penny shot me a look which could only be interpreted as "Oh yes, Mr English Teacher, and I thought we weren't supposed to use that sort of language".

But it was too late. The simile was already out of the bag, and Dionysis pounced on it before I had a chance to explain.

'So you have your own bridge in England, do you?' he said, clearly but erroneously impressed.

'No, not at all. It's just an expression which means that—'

'And that is why you're going back to England? To paint this bridge of yours?'

To Penny's obvious amusement, I floundered to come up with an explanation of what the phrase means, and eventually Dionysis seemed to understand. Or so I thought.

After we'd come back from the UK, Dionysis and his family invited us to their traditional Easter Sunday celebrations, which was really quite an honour. However, after lunch, I was sitting having a drink with Dionysis and some of his brothers-in-law (he has several) when he suddenly announced, 'Robert has his own bridge in England, you know.'

Five pairs of eyes popped in surprise.

'No, no,' I began, but Dionysis was warming to his theme.

'Yes,' he said, 'and he had to go back to England recently to paint it.'

I tried to interject and disabuse Dionysis and his

148

brothers-in-law of the idea that Penny and I must be incredibly wealthy if we could afford to own an entire bridge, but by now, the floodgates were open, and I was bombarded with questions.

'So how big *is* this bridge?' asked one brother-in-law.

'Well, it's about two and a half kilometres long, I think, but we don't actually—'

'Wow,' said another brother-in-law. 'That's nearly as big as the Rio Bridge.'

'Yes, but—'

'How many litres of paint do you need?'

'The thing is, you see, we—'

'What colour do you paint it?'

'No, you don't underst—'

'Do you do all the work yourselves or do you have help?'

As if my awkward embarrassment couldn't have got any more acute, Dionysis then threw in that this was our "fourth" road bridge.

Eyes popped even wider.

'You have three other bridges?'

'But painting just one of them must be a never-ending job.'

I attempted to explain that this was pretty much the point of what I'd been trying to convey in the first place, but I was interrupted by one of the brothers-in-law insisting that everyone drink a toast to 'Robert and Penny's road bridges!'

Penny, of course, has never let me forget the Forth Road Bridge fiasco, and since then, I've never once dared to pick her up on her use of even the most obscure of English idioms. With what I consider to be one of the cruelest of ironies, though, I've since discovered that a far more durable paint has been developed which means that, in future, the Forth Road Bridge will only need to be repainted once in every twenty-five years. So, there's another stitch lost from the rich tapestry of the English language, albeit a potentially rather confusing one.

21

Smelly Thursday
and Satan Incarnate

Since I mentioned Easter in the previous chapter, I may as well go with the flow and say a few words about how this is celebrated in Greece and other related matters. The first related matter is that last year (2016), Good Friday in Greece was about a month later than Good Friday in the UK because Western Christian churches and Eastern Orthodox churches calculate the date differently. The former use the Gregorian calendar, while the latter use the Julian calendar, so Easter can fall at any time between 22nd March and 8th May depending on which calendar is used. My calendar is from the World Wildlife Fund, so I've no idea when Easter's supposed to be. Somewhere during the month where there's a picture of a fluffy bunny rabbit, I suppose.

It's always puzzled me that nobody seems to have much idea of the date when Jesus died, but they seem very clear on exactly when he was born. It doesn't matter what calendar you buy, Christmas Day is always on 25th December, Jesus being born very conveniently slap bang in the middle of a three day Bank Holiday. But when was the crucifixion? March, April, Mayish sort of time?

Since Easter is such a moveable feast, several of the days before and after Easter Sunday have to have special names because you can't just say, 'Oh yes, we always go to church on 18th April every year.' This wouldn't make much sense, so you have to say Palm Sunday, which is the Sunday before Easter Sunday, and in Eastern Christianity is the day after Lazarus Saturday. Then in Western Christianity you've got days like Maundy Thursday and Good Friday.

You've also got the intriguingly named Spy Wednesday, which is apparently so called because that was the day Judas Iscariot did his deal with the Sanhedrin to rat on Jesus for thirty pieces of silver. But why "spy"? Judas was hardly a spy. Jesus knew exactly what he was. A snitch, a squealer, a stoolie, a narc – even a tittle-tattle, but surely not a spy. It would make far more sense to call it something like Supergrass Wednesday rather than Spy Wednesday.

Fortunately, it's quite a bit simpler in Greece where Easter Week is just *Megáli Evdomáda* – "Big Week" – and the days are just called Big Monday, Big Tuesday and so on. Lent is a little different, though, as the Greeks have what they call *Kathará Theftéra* or "Clean Monday", which marks the beginning of forty days of fasting before Easter (*Páscha*). Forty days? And people do it voluntarily? They'd be force-feeding hunger strikers through a tube long before that.

In reality, however, hardly anyone tries to do Lent on a few sips of water a day, but a lot of Greeks do seem to abstain from eating meat. And to prepare for six weeks of a souvlaki-free diet, they have what's called *Tsiknopémpti* on the Thursday before Lent. This is when most Greek people stuff their faces with as much meat as they can lay their hands on – or I should say as much as many of them can afford these days. I've heard some Greeks refer to *Tsiknopémpti* as "Smelly Thursday", which I initially thought was a reference to the – how shall I put this? – aromas emanating from certain orifices as a result of an overindulgence in meat-eating. Almost disappointingly, though, I later discovered that the smell they're talking about is actually the smell of meat being cooked rather than the – well, I'm sure you get the point by now.

Easter in Greece is much more important than Christmas. This is the direct opposite of Britain where Christmas cards and all the other tinselly paraphernalia start appearing in the shops as early as August, accompanied by endlessly piped carols and other Christmas "hits" like the heart-stoppingly dreadful *The Little Drummer Boy* and *I Wish It Could Be Christmas Every Day-ee-ay*. If shops in Britain get their way, it very soon will be Christmas every day-ee-ay. Roy Wood, you should be ashamed of yourself. I mean, you expect this kind of drivel from the likes of Cliff Richard and his vomit-inducing *Mistletoe and Wine*, but surely not from the man who created such great songs as *See My Baby Jive*.

Okay, sorry for the mini rant there, but perhaps you'll understand my venomous response to Christmas muzak better when I tell you that I once worked in a large department store during the Yuletide shopping frenzy – one of my many temporary jobs in the past – and I was inflicted with this musical equivalent of waterboarding for eight solid hours a day. It was all right for the customers. At least they could escape after twenty minutes or so. As for me, I used to have to go home every night and listen to three Leonard Cohen albums on the trot to cheer myself up.

At least in Greece they don't start all the Christmas nonsense until a respectably short time before the big event itself, but even that seems to be creeping earlier and earlier these days.

Anyway, back to Easter in Greece...

About half of the Greek population of nearly eleven

million live in Athens, but during the Easter holiday many of these return to the towns and villages they came from originally to celebrate with their extended families. The highlight of the festivities is lunch on Easter Sunday when they all get together to feast on the lamb they've been roasting on a spit since early in the morning. It's very much a family thing, so we felt very honoured when the family who runs our local olive press invited us to join them on our second Easter in Greece. (See previous chapter regarding my Forth Road Bridge gaffe.)

Having been a vegetarian for over twenty-five years by then, I managed to avert my eyes from the lamb which was slowly revolving on the spit, its teeth bared in a kind of insane grin and its eyeballs protruding wildly out of its roasted skull, but the smell was inescapable. Then there was the *kokorétsı*, which is considered to be a great delicacy and only eaten on special occasions like Easter. According to one recipe I came across, the main ingredients are: "Guts of lamb. You might need guts from more than one lamb. Ask for two hearts, two spleen, liver and one lung, two testicles. Bowels of lamb. At least four are required for a medium size *kokorétsı*". But just the two testicles, eh?

And here's an extract from the recipe instructions: "Start skewering the guts onto the *soúvla* – the iron stick used for roasting. Pin one end of the first bowel in the one side of the *soúvla* and wind the intestine around the skewer. If the bowel reaches its end, tie it with the end of the next bowel and continue to wind until all bowels are wrapped and no guts are visible (you should only see the bowels along the *soúvla*)". Mmm. Nice. Now that really would cause Irritable Bowel Syndrome.

The weather was fine that particular Easter Sunday at the family home way up in the mountains, so tables were arranged in a long row in the courtyard, and when about thirty-odd people sat down to eat, I found myself sitting

154

next to a fairly elderly *papás* – a Greek Orthodox priest. He looked me up and down a couple of times and then asked me if I was German. (In this area of Greece, people tend to assume that if you're not Greek, you're probably German.) After I told him I was English, he asked if I was Catholic.

'No,' I said.

'Are you Protestant?'

I told him I wasn't and half expected his next question would be whether I was animal, vegetable or mineral. Instead, he asked me if I was religious *at all*.

When I said I didn't really subscribe to any particular religion, he nodded as if to convey that this was perfectly acceptable, but then he pointed at the plate in front of me, which was laden with salad, cheese and other veggie stuff.

'But you have no meat,' he said with obvious astonishment and seemed to be about to summon someone to rectify this oversight.

'Er, no,' I said. 'I'm actually vegetarian.'

The priest threw up his hands in horror, and by the look on his face it was as if I'd just told him I was Satan incarnate or one of the Four Horsemen of the Apocalypse. I'm pretty sure it was as much as he could do to stop himself making the sign of the cross. Apparently, it was okay to be bordering on atheist, but being vegetarian was a sin far worse than anything Vlad the Impaler could ever have dreamed up. As far as I remember, the priest didn't really say much to me after that.

I also seem to remember that Penny and I went home that night and watched all four-and-a-half hours of *The Greatest Story Ever Told* on the telly. This is hardly surprising in a way because during the couple of weeks up to and including Easter, all of the Greek TV channels show almost nothing else but films about Jesus.

Sometimes, though, the Jesus link is rather tenuous to say the least. The problem is that there are so many viewing hours to fill and so many channels that they can't all show the same movies, so they end up seriously scraping the barrel. I can imagine some vigorous head scratching in the programming departments of the TV stations when they're planning their Easter schedules:

PROGRAMMER 1:   What about *Spartacus* then?

PROGRAMMER 2:   *Spartacus*? You mean the one with Kirk Douglas and all the "I am Spartacus, no I'm Spartacus" business?

PROGRAMMER 1:   That's the one, yeah.

PROGRAMMER 2:   Jesus in that one, is he?

PROGRAMMER 1:   Don't think so, no. But there's lots of Roman centurions in it though.

PROGRAMMER 2:   Fair enough. Stick it on the list then.

As a final note about Easter in Greece, there are a few customary phrases that the foreign visitor might find useful to know. In the run-up to Easter (i.e. during Big Week), you'll often hear people greeting each other with '*Kaló Páscha*' ("Happy Easter"), but as soon as Easter has been and gone, this changes to '*chrónia pollá*'. Literally, it means "many years" or "many happy returns" as we'd say in the UK. On Easter Sunday itself and for a few days afterwards, people often greet you with '*Christós anésti*' – "Christ has risen" – and the standard response is '*Alithós anésti*' – "Truly he was resurrected". I got this a bit wrong one Easter when someone said '*Christós anésti*' to me and, without thinking, I replied, '*Epeísis*', which is what you usually say to most other greetings such as '*Na eíste kalá*' – "Be well" – or '*Kalí evdomáda*' – "Have a good week".

Epeísis means something like "You too", but in this context was totally inappropriate because what I'd effectively said in response to this guy's 'Christ has risen' was 'And so have you!' I got rather a strange look for that one.

22

One Baptism and a Funeral

Religion in Greece is far more important than it is in Britain with about 90% of the population being members of the Greek Orthodox Church. It doesn't take a mathematical genius to work out that all other religions are therefore very much in the minority, and although all are tolerated, the Orthodox Church is particularly sniffy about Roman Catholicism. This apparently began with the Great Schism of 1054, the reasons for which I don't intend to go into here, mainly because I don't really understand most of them.

However, to give just one example of how Catholicism is generally viewed in Greece, the son of some friends of ours was recently given a school homework assignment to "Give twenty-six reasons why Roman Catholicism is wrong". Not "Describe the differences between Greek Orthodoxy and Roman Catholicism" but why Catholicism is *wrong*. And whoever the teacher was that set this assignment, they obviously had a very specific idea as to precisely how many reasons there were for Catholicism's wrong-headedness.

So entrenched is the Orthodox Church in Greek society that religious icons are everywhere – in shops, bars, restaurants and offices as well as people's homes – and are usually small paintings on wood of Christ, the Virgin Mary or some saint or other. Per capita, these icons probably outnumber all of the Manchester United and boy band posters to be found in the UK by a ratio of about twenty to one.

There are more churches in Greece than you could shake a tanker-load of holy water at, and many of them are so small that there's only just enough room for the priest and a congregation of two or three at a pinch. Many are built in barely accessible locations such as the tops of mountains or on tiny islands and only have one service a year, generally on the day of the saint that the church was named after.

Almost everyone in Greece has a "name day" (*onomastikí eortí*) since almost everyone in Greece has the same first name as a saint. So, for instance, Yiorgos's (George's) Day is 23rd April and Sofia's Day is 17th September. But if your name is Panagiotis, you have a choice of three days on which to celebrate your name day. This is because there are so many Panagiotises, the bars and tavernas wouldn't be able to cope if they all tried to celebrate at once. For similar reasons, there are two name days for women called Maria, although they don't get to choose because 15th August is for married Marias and 21st November is for unmarried Marias.

It's a tradition that the person whose name day it is pays for all the drinks and food, which is why I'm convinced that a lot of people never venture outside their homes when their day comes around. Fortunately, I don't have this problem myself as there's never been a Saint Robert, although All Saints' Day (*Ton Agíon Pánton*) is apparently also designated as the Name Day For People Who Don't Have Name Days. A Greek friend once suggested that I should try and get myself canonised so that there'd be a proper Saint Robert's Day, but I pointed out that: a) I'm not too hot on the performing miracles front; and b) I'm not overly keen on dying a premature and excruciatingly painful death, which seems to be almost *de rigueur* for a lot of saints.

Although there's never been a Robert who's been considered sufficiently worthy of sainthood, there is however a Saint Penelope so Penny does have a name day, which is on 1st September. I do find it somewhat ironic that Saint Penelope also happens to be the patron saint of police officers in Greece, but Penny would doubtless disagree.

Despite Penny and I not being great churchgoers ourselves, we have attended a few Greek Orthodox services, and they seem to be a lot less formal than church services in the UK. At baptisms, for instance, the service is quite long, so it's perfectly acceptable for members of the congregation to nip outside the church every now and then for a quick smoke and a natter.

We also had to go to a funeral a couple of years ago, so I dug out my old black tie and suit (bought for a fiver from Oxfam twenty years ago for a similar occasion), and Penny put on a much more recently purchased black dress. But as we drove into the village where the funeral service was being held, we noticed that none of the people making their way to the church were wearing black apart from a handful of elderly women. (It's traditional in Greece – although less observed now – that when a man dies, their widow wears only black for the rest of their lives.) Almost all of the men were smartly but casually dressed in jeans and T-shirts, and it was the first time in my life that I'd ever felt over-dressed.

I was going to stick out like a sore thumb in my suit, but there was no time to go home and change so dispensing with the jacket and the tie was the best I could do in order not to draw attention to myself. Who knows? Maybe wearing a black suit and tie to a Greek funeral is considered the height of bad taste and even grossly disrespectful to the deceased and the bereaved family. I certainly wasn't going to take the risk, and as it turned out, my open-necked white shirt and black trousers went totally unremarked. Penny of course had had no option but to stick with her black dress unless she'd stripped down to her underwear, and I'm absolutely certain that would have raised a few eyebrows – disapproving or otherwise.

Even the major services on the Christian calendar are relatively informal affairs in Greek Orthodox churches, and Midnight Mass on Easter Saturday is no exception. We'd been told that this was an experience not to be missed, so along we went to the church in our local village. It was quite literally packed to overflowing, and there was an almost carnival-type atmosphere despite the incessant monotone wailing of the priests. For me, though, the real highlight came at the end of the service when we all lit a candle each and then had to carry them home without letting the flame go out. Apparently, if you achieve this, you'll have good luck for the rest of the year, but quite the opposite if the candle flame is extinguished on the way. Since our house is a good ten minute drive from the church, Penny and I decided to compromise and see if we could get our candles as far as the nearest taverna, less than two hundred yards away.

We failed.

Even cupping a hand around the flame to protect it from the light breeze, we'd barely gone twenty yards before both our candles spluttered and died. Having relit them, we set off again, more slowly this time, but the damned things went out another three or four times before we reached the breezeless haven of the taverna.

That was about ten years ago, and I'm still not sure whether you add on another year of bad luck for each time your candle goes out, but I can certainly point to a number of occasions in the ensuing years when luck was definitely not on our side. If we ever try the Easter candle thing again, I'm taking some of those trick birthday cake candles that, once lit, are impossible to blow out.

23

Unlucky for Some

Of course, I'm not by any means the first person to have remarked on the links between religion and superstition, but the Easter Saturday candle episode seemed to be a particular case in point. It also epitomises how the vast majority of Greeks can be members of the Orthodox Church whilst simultaneously being seriously superstitious. And I do mean *seriously*. Anybody who's ever visited Greece will have seen the extraordinary array of talismans for sale to ward off the evil eye (*mátiasma*), which is feared by almost everyone in the country. Attracting the attention of the evil eye can cause all kinds of unpleasantness to happen to you and is most likely to occur if you make the gods envious in some way, such as when someone pays you a compliment. (Interestingly, it seems perfectly possible to fear the ancient "gods", plural, whilst still believing in the "one true God" of Christianity.)

Fortunately, there are a number of ways to keep the evil eye at bay. The most popular is to wear some article like a pendant or bracelet with a *matáki* on it – a blue eye which reflects the evil away from you. For added protection, you can also wear your underwear inside-out. Garlic is another effective method for warding off the evil eye, and if you don't happen to have any on you when someone pays you a compliment, whispering "*skórdo*" – the Greek word for garlic – and spitting on yourself three times is supposed to do the trick. By spitting, I don't mean a real heavy phlegm clearance but more of a symbolic "ftou ftou ftou".

But symbolic or not, the first time Penny and I came across this was when we told a friend how beautiful her newborn baby was, and she immediately spat on the kid three times. Maria obviously clocked the look of astonishment on our faces and quickly explained about not wanting to attract the attention of the evil eye. I felt it only fair to warn her not to do the same thing in public if she was ever in the UK because it would be the attention of a child protection agency she'd be attracting, and this could potentially cause a lot more problems than anything the evil eye could throw at her.

The bad news – or even worse news – about the evil eye is that however many of these precautions you take, it can sometimes still find a way of breaking through your defences. But all is not lost even if this happens because throughout Greece there are those who have the ability to release others from the effects of the evil eye. This is usually done by reciting a special prayer over the afflicted person, although the exact wording of the prayer can only be passed from a man to a woman, or vice versa, and only on Good Friday.

There are probably many people in our area who know this prayer, but there's only one that I'm aware of, and she worked as a cook at our local taverna. According to Tom and Nuala, who used to run the taverna, people would frequently turn up to seek out this woman and ask her to relieve whatever suffering it was that the evil eye had inflicted upon them. This would often turn out to be little more than a headache or some other minor ailment such as a prolonged bout of yawning since there are plenty of Greeks – mostly among the older generations – who blame almost every misfortune that befalls them on the evil eye. The cook was therefore never short of people asking her to work her "magic", although this inevitably meant that the taverna's customers sometimes had to wait a little longer for their souvlakis.

Some Greek superstitions are the same as ones we have in the UK, but there are also variations. Here, it's *Tuesday* the thirteenth which is unlucky and not Friday the thirteenth, which is possibly to avoid spoiling the start of an otherwise perfectly enjoyable weekend. Another difference – although not exactly a superstition – is that cats in Greece only have seven lives instead of the British cats' nine. This is perhaps yet another example of Greek austerity cuts but also demonstrates that it's much better to be a cat in Britain than in Greece.

Finally, there's also a Greek superstition that sprinkling salt behind the backs of unwelcome guests will cause them to leave almost immediately. This is why whenever the Troika visits – they're the unholy triumvirate of European and IMF officials who periodically come to Greece to check that the government is carrying out its orders to impoverish Greek citizens – you often see people following them round with wheelbarrows loaded to the brim with salt.

I'm actually very sympathetic towards the Greek obsession with superstitions as I'm pretty superstitious myself. I even invented one of my own once, and it involves automatic washing machines. Penny caught me in the act of carrying out this particular superstition very early on in our relationship, which almost brought the relationship to an abrupt and rather premature end. I'd just loaded the washing machine and pressed the start button when she came into the kitchen.

'Why are you standing on one leg in front of the washing machine?' she asked, perhaps not unreasonably.

'I'm waiting for the water to start filling,' I said, thinking that this was a perfectly logical reason.

'Er, why?'

'Because after you press the start button, you have to stand on one leg until you hear the water coming into the drum. Only then can you put your foot back down.'

Judging by the blank expression I got in return, I realised that further explanation was necessary.

'It's bad luck if you don't.'

'What sort of bad luck?' she said.

'I'm not really sure,' I said, 'but I certainly don't want to risk finding out.'

Then, pausing only to give me one of those looks which said "Look, as a fully qualified psychological therapist, it's my considered opinion that you're in serious need of professional help", she left the room.

Apart from almost ending our relationship, another slight drawback of my washing machine superstition emerged some time after we moved to Greece. Our washing machine here is in an outbuilding, but the stopcock for the water is outside and round the corner, and on one occasion, I'd forgotten to turn the stopcock on before I pressed the start button. Having already assumed the one-legged position, I obviously had no choice but to hop several yards to rectify the situation. On the way back – and still on one leg until I could verify that the washing machine was indeed beginning to fill with water – I almost tripped over one of the dogs and could easily have broken my ankle in the process. I'm pretty sure that if I hadn't observed the standing on one leg superstition, I'd *definitely* have broken it.

I've no idea quite why I decided to invent a new superstition, particularly when I already have to spend more than enough time walking round ladders, informing people of the perils of opening an umbrella indoors, and trying to remember which door I came in at so I can make sure I exit by the same one. However, I do feel a warm glow at the thought that one day I might walk into a laundrette and find a whole row of people standing on one leg in front of a bank of washing machines. In fact, this may not be entirely beyond the realms of possibility since the daughter of some friends was at school here in Greece a few years ago and the teacher asked each member of the class to describe a superstition. And yes, she told all her fellow students about the importance of standing on one leg while you're waiting for the water to start filling the washing machine. Result!

Besides inventing new superstitions, I'm always keen to discover any that I haven't come across before so I can be forewarned and take the necessary defensive action. Every so often, though, there's a possibility that the defensive action can do more harm than whatever the evil is that it's designed to ward off. Take, for instance, the time many years ago when I lived on my own for a few months. It's a well known superstition that if you drop a knife on the floor, you mustn't pick it up yourself but get someone else to do it. However, after having dropped every knife in the house during this period of solitary existence, it became extremely dangerous to walk across the kitchen floor, especially in bare feet. Not only that, but I ended up having to butter my toast with a garden trowel.

Most of my friends and family are heavily scornful of my belief in superstitions, although there has been the odd occasion when I've been able to demonstrate the potentially catastrophic consequences of their scepticism. To give just one example, when our friends Huw and Julie came to visit us in Greece, we went for a meal one evening at a taverna in a fairly remote village up in the hills. While we were eating, I noticed that Huw and Julie were both eating off two plates. That is, each of them had an empty plate underneath the one their food was on, and I pointed out that this could bring them all kinds of bad luck. As so often in such cases, my friendly warning didn't simply go unheeded, it was also met with much derisive laughter and comments of the "Don't be so ridiculous" variety. But I was to have the last laugh.

On the way home after the meal, Huw was driving the car they'd hired while they were staying with us and was pulled over by the police for a spot check. Even though Huw had only had about half a bottle of beer with the meal, the cops must have smelt it on his breath, so they breathalysed him. The test came up clear, but the cops were obviously unhappy about this, and they tried three more times before finally having to admit that Huw wasn't over the limit and let us go on our way. (A Greek friend told us later that the reason for having to take so many tests was because the breathalyser equipment the local police use is so old that they don't trust it to give an accurate reading. They've sometimes breathalysed people who've been too drunk even to stand, and the test has still said they were under the limit.)

Okay, so Huw didn't get busted that night, but would the police have pulled him over in the first place if he hadn't been eating off two plates a short time before? And that wasn't the end of the story either. Huw and Julie left us the next morning on their way back to the island of Zakynthos, dropped their hire car off at the mainland port of Kyllini and hopped on the ferry. During their one-hour trip across the short stretch of sea, there was a not insignificant earthquake almost directly beneath the boat, and when they arrived on Zakynthos, they discovered that there was a taxi drivers' strike. This meant that they had to find alternative means of getting to the apartment they'd been renting, so they got on a bus. But it was the wrong one, and it was heading in the exact opposite direction to where they wanted to go. By the time they found a bus to take them back again, the trip from the port to their apartment had taken them almost three hours instead of the normal fifteen-minute taxi ride.

Despite what I consider to be overwhelming evidence to the contrary, Huw and Julie continued to insist that none of these events had occurred purely because they'd eaten off two plates. There's just no telling people sometimes.

But whether or not eating off two plates really does bring bad luck, why take the risk? I wouldn't even chance it with our dogs and cats in case something dreadful might happen to them. Only the other night, for instance, I went to feed one of the cats and realised I'd put her plate of food down on top of an empty one. I whipped it back off immediately of course because even if they aren't superstitious themselves, it's quite likely that cats – black or otherwise – are affected by good and bad luck in the same way as we are. This is why I've never taught any of our pets how to use the washing machine because trying to get them to stand on one leg would be an absolute nightmare.

24

Cats and Dogs
and Chicken Guards

Cats. Where would we be without them, eh? We got our two – Ella and the imaginatively named Stripy Cat – soon after we moved in to Xerika, having been advised that they'd be essential for keeping down the mice, rat and possibly even snake populations. Good advice in principle, although Ella in particular seems to have got it into her head from an early stage that *relocating* small mammals is sometimes preferable to actually killing them. Normally, I'd find this highly commendable except that, more often than not, her idea of relocating mice and other small creatures is to bring them into the house alive and then let them go. However, Penny and I cottoned on a long time ago that when Ella miaows to come in, we usually know if she's got a "gift" for us because her miaow sounds more like a very small donkey trying to impersonate quite a large frog, so the door stays shut.

I'd never really had much to do with cats before we moved to Greece, having been far more of a "dog person", but I soon became very fond of our two, despite their irritating habits. Apart from Ella bringing live animals into the house – including small snakes on a couple of occasions – they both insist on coming indoors to use their litter tray even when it's a perfectly fine day and they have acres of space to choose from outside.

Then there's the tablet issue. Most people who have cats will already know that it's virtually impossible to get a cat to take any kind of oral medication by prising their jaws open and trying to ram a tablet down their throat. Empirical evidence clearly demonstrates that this method will invariably result in a lot of blood being spilt – all of it your own – from several brutally inflicted bites and scratches. So what's the alternative? Crush the tablet into the finest of powders and thoroughly mix it into a bowlful of the tastiest, most expensive cat food ever made? Forget it. One sniff and the cat'll turn to you with a curled lip and arched eyebrows and an expression which can only be interpreted as: "Do I look stupid? Well, do I? I think we both know who's the stupid one round here, don't we? Spending all that money and then ruining a perfectly good meal by criminally adulterating it with a load of foul-smelling, poisonous filth that I wouldn't even give to a dog?"

And what about the staring? That really freaks me out, that does. And they always choose the worst possible moment to do it – usually when Penny's gone back to the UK for a few days and I'm here on my own, miles from anywhere, and it's late at night. There I'll be, watching the telly with one of the cats purring contentedly on my lap, when all of a sudden and for no apparent reason, the purring stops abruptly, the cat's head shoots up like a rocket-propelled periscope, and it stares wide-eyed with horror at "something" behind me. I snap my head round, my heart pounding as I brace myself for the sight of the most terrifying thing that I've ever seen in my life and – nothing but empty air. I turn back to the cat with a 'What was that all about?', but she just gives me the feline equivalent of a shrug, then curls herself back into a ball, purring even more loudly than before. In fact, I'm almost certain that it sounds more like sniggering than purring.

As I said earlier, I've always been more of a dog person myself, and at the last count, Penny and I have five of them, although at one time we had seven dogs and three cats. We never meant to have quite so many dogs, and we certainly don't go looking for them. All but one of our current dogs simply turned up at our gate, apparently wanting a home. Not *en masse*, of course, but individually over a period of about a year. There are a lot of strays in Greece, and my guess is that word got round on some kind of canine grapevine that there were a couple of soft Brits living halfway up a mountain who would take in any dog that happened to turn up on their doorstep.

Including the five we have now and also Bessie, the Staffordshire Bull Terrier we brought with us from England, we've had fourteen dogs living with us in the thirteen years we've been at Xerika. Five of those who are no longer with us died from eating poisoned meat, which quite a lot of Greek farmers put out to kill foxes. Even though our land is all fenced off, the fencing itself is quite ancient now, and as fast as we can plug any escape holes, the dogs will open up a new one. Five acres to do what they like in, and they still want the rest of the countryside to explore. Usually, they come back within an hour or two unless they've eaten some of the poisoned meat that's been scattered around the neighbourhood. On several occasions, Petros, our local vet, has managed to save some of our dogs when they've been poisoned, but it depends on how much they've eaten and how quickly we can get them to his surgery.

Nor is it only farmers who litter the countryside with poisoned meat. Hunters do it as well, and although the intention is also to kill foxes, their motive is different. Whereas the farmers want to protect their chickens and

172

other livestock, the hunters' justification is to stop the foxes killing the local wildlife. 'After all,' they say, 'if we let all these foxes run round killing all the rabbits and hares and so on, there wouldn't be anything left for us to shoot at, would there?'

Hunting is extremely popular in Greece, and during the hunting season you might be forgiven for thinking you'd found yourself in the middle of a war zone. Apart from the almost relentless barrage of gunfire, nearly every hunter you see is dressed from head to toe in full camouflage gear as if they were competing in a Rambo lookalike contest. Apparently, this is essential if you're to stand any chance of winning the heroic battle against the vicious hordes of very small birds that are often no bigger than sparrows.

The attitude of many Greeks towards animals is something that we found very hard to come to terms with when we moved here. The first time we walked Bessie through the town on a lead, for instance, a little boy was so alarmed that he threw a lump of wood at her. In all seriousness, in a rural area like this, nobody would have raised so much as an eyebrow if it had been a pig or a goat we'd had on a lead. To be fair to the boy, though, and to all the other Greeks who have a less than exemplary attitude towards animals, it really doesn't help that the Orthodox Church teaches that animals don't have souls, so it's pretty much okay to treat them as badly as you like.

I'm glad to say, however, that things have improved considerably since our early days in Greece. More and more now, there are adverts for dog food and treats on the TV as well as soft toy dogs and other animals in the shops. It's also noticeable that there's been a major increase in people bringing their pets to Petros's surgery for routine vaccinations, checkups and even grooming. Ten years or so ago, the vast majority of Petros's clients were farmers with sick goats or chickens, their motivation being entirely financial rather than concern for the animals' wellbeing.

There's still plenty of room for improvement in the way animals are treated in Greece, and even though there are laws in place for the prevention of cruelty, they rarely seem to be applied. The widespread farmers' practice of keeping a dog permanently tied up – supposedly to guard their chickens against foxes – continues almost unabated despite being outlawed a few years ago.

These dogs spend their entire lives being restricted to the same small patch of ground, the size of which is determined by the length of their chains. They're often only fed on the occasional lump of stale bread, and they're frequently left without water or shade even during the hottest months of the summer. It's always struck me as absurd why farmers imagine for one moment that these dogs are any kind of deterrent to a fox that's determined to have chicken for its supper. The fox, being one of the smartest creatures on the planet, is going to realise very quickly that the dog's movement is limited by the length of its tether, so will simply circumvent it in order to get to its prey.

One of our own dogs was a "chicken guard" when we first came across her tied to a length of rope on a small farm about a mile from our place. But being a lot brighter than many other dogs in her predicament – or perhaps because she hadn't yet lost the will to live like they probably had – she often used to chew through her rope and make her escape. Several times, she'd turn up on our land and spend a couple of hours or so playing with our own dogs before heading off back to her chickens. Maybe she wasn't as bright as we'd thought, or maybe she felt a genuine responsibility for the chickens under her protection, or otherwise she wouldn't have gone back at all. But whatever the reason, Girlie (another imaginative name) obviously didn't just "play" with our dogs when she came to visit because one day she appeared at Xerika with two very young puppies in tow, both of whom bore a striking resemblance to our Rory. And this time, she stayed for good.

Well, not quite for good. A couple of years after she'd moved in, she suddenly disappeared, and although we scoured the area for several days, she was nowhere to be found. Eventually, we gave up looking for her, sadly resigning ourselves to the likelihood that she too had met her death from eating poison. But a couple of days later, we heard her unmistakable barking at the gate, and we rushed to let her in. She didn't seem too much the worse for wear, but she had a short length of twine attached to her collar. The free end looked like it had been chewed through, so the most likely explanation for her disappearance was that somebody had grabbed her and tied her up, but whoever it was hadn't reckoned on her abilities as an escapologist.

The very next day, we found out exactly who it was that had abducted her when a fairly elderly Greek couple turned up and excitedly started pointing at Girlie through the wire mesh of the gate. They both spoke in Greek at the same time and with the speed of a hyperactive machine gun, so Penny and I could hardly understand a word they were saying. It became clear after a while, however, that they were claiming that Girlie was *their* dog and we had stolen her from them. We told them this was nonsense, of course, but they were adamant that they'd had Girlie for at least a year.

The argument was getting out of hand, partly because neither side could understand much of what the other was saying, so I rang Petros in desperation to ask him to translate. Passing the phone back and forth between us and the Greek couple, we asked them why they wanted

Girlie so badly when there were plenty of stray dogs around that they could use as a chicken guard if they insisted on having one at all.

'Because she eats very little,' they said.

It was about the only true thing they'd come out with so far. Girlie has always had a small appetite, so it was pretty clear that these people wanted her because she'd be cheap to maintain.

'What do I say to them?' I asked Petros, who was not only our vet but also a good friend by now. 'They're still standing here, ranting on about Girlie belonging to them.'

'They're obviously trying to pull a fast one,' he said. 'Just tell them to f*** off.'

Sound advice, I thought, but diplomatically deciding not to use Petros's exact words, Penny and I simply said goodbye to the Greek couple and walked away from the gate. Back inside the house, we kept a careful watch through the window to make sure they didn't try and make a grab for Girlie, but instead, they stood arguing with each other for a few seconds and then stomped off up the track.

Perhaps rather naively, we thought this would be the last we'd ever hear of them, but the following day, we got a call from Petros.

'Their son's just been in to my surgery, and he's threatening to report you to the police for stealing their dog.'

'Oh God,' I said. 'So now what do we do?'

'No problem,' said Petros. 'I told him you'd had Girlie microchipped a couple of years ago, so you could prove you were the legal owners.'

'But we've never had any of our dogs chipped.'

'I know. Just bring her in now and I'll do it straight away. The only thing is, there's a certificate that goes with the microchip, and it has to be dated the same day as I implant it.'

'So it won't prove that we had Girlie before today.'

'It will if I backdate it three years,' he said, and I could hear him grinning as he spoke.

We never heard another word from the Girlie-snatchers, and Girlie herself is still with us and clearly enjoying her retirement from her life as a chicken guard.

25

I'd Rather Eat My Own Face

Most Greek farmers only keep chickens for their own use and perhaps make a few extra euros selling eggs that are surplus to requirements. Olive oil is a different matter altogether, and according to the official figures for 2015, accounted for 15% of Greece's entire agricultural output and 21.4% of all the olive oil produced by EU member states. In the area where we live, almost everyone has olive trees, ranging from a dozen or so that have been passed down through the generations to much larger commercial holdings of three or four thousand.

Penny and I have four hundred and twenty on our land, and at the time of writing it's six months, three weeks, four days, sixteen hours and twenty-eight minutes until we begin this year's harvest in November. Not that I'm wishing my life away counting down the time in eager anticipation until I can get out there with my olive-whacking stick. Totally the opposite, in fact. This will be our fourteenth season, and I dread the prospect more and more every year. Now I know what to expect, the dread begins earlier and earlier. Last year, the night sweats started as early as the middle of June.

For those who've never witnessed or taken part in an olive harvest, this is what you do:

1. Place large nets on the ground under the trees.

2. Whack hell out of the trees so that the olives fall onto the nets.
3. Cut out some of the branches as you go.
4. Transfer the olives from the nets into sacks.
5. Send the sacks to the olive press.

All sounds straightforward enough, doesn't it? But don't be fooled. The olive harvest is, in reality, not only sheer bloody hard work and mind-numbingly tedious to boot, but it's also an activity which should be registered with the Dangerous Sports Association. Take the harvest three years ago, for instance. On the very first day, I had to go to the local hospital as I had a fragment of olive leaf lodged in my eye from looking up into a tree whilst bashing it with my stick. This meant that I had to wear an eye patch for the next twenty-four hours, which seriously affected my whacking aim. Not long afterwards, I almost took my leg off with a chainsaw.

I had various pulled muscles from lifting sacks of olives and slipping on greasy olive nets, and it took about eight months to recover from olive harvesters' elbow – in both elbows, I might add. I've had numerous cuts, grazes and bruises from falling out of the trees, and I've suffered mild concussion on several occasions from bashing my head on an overhanging branch. Combine all this with the detrimental effect on my liver (caused by having to consume several pints of beer every night to ease the pain), and you'll understand why I believe olive harvesting is far more dangerous than jumping the Grand Canyon with jet-propelled roller skates during a force ten gale and with a king cobra down each trouser leg.

As well as the physical danger, there is also the serious risk of the total disintegration of relationships. Penny and I have exactly the same argument every harvest on an almost daily (and sometimes hourly) basis:

PENNY: Okay, this tree's done. Next one.

179

ME:	But there's more olives up there than you could shake a stick at.
PENNY:	There's about twelve.
ME:	Couple more bashes, that's all.
PENNY:	We don't have the time.

At about this point in the argument, Penny usually accuses me of being anally retentive. I then retaliate by telling her she's slapdash and wasteful, and then we end up not speaking for hours. (Why is it that airheaded, disorganised people always accuse efficient and well-organised people of being anally retentive? This thought could lead me on to consider what the opposite of anally retentive might be, but perhaps I won't go there just now.)

I have spoken to a number of friends in Britain who have never even seen an olive tree, never mind harvested one, and they all have this absurdly romantic image of what it's like. They seem to have the idea that Penny and I stroll out into the olive grove every bright and sunny morning, each with a little wicker basket over one arm, and spend a delightful day casually plucking individual olives from the trees and singing cheery olive harvesting songs. Come to think of it, I've never heard *anyone* singing while they're harvesting – cheerily or otherwise. I have, on the other hand, heard an awful lot of swearing, groaning, sighing and moaning.

Now, I'm totally against the idea of genetically modifying crops (or anything else for that matter), but in the case of olive trees, I would be prepared to make an exception. My brother-in-law Chris and I discussed this once during one of his visits here and decided that it shouldn't be beyond the wit of some scientist or other to design the GM Self-Harvesting Olive. This would be achieved by equipping each olive with its own tiny machete, which it would use to cut through its stalk and detach itself from the tree. It could also have a mini parachute so that the fruit would not be bruised when it hit the ground, and it would have little legs to enable it to walk to the nearest sack and climb into it. Until that glorious day comes, however, I will have to endure several months of nightmares about the impending harvest and then the pure hell of the harvest itself.

Incidentally, when I mentioned the GM Self-Harvesting Olive in one of my podcast episodes, a friend called Penny Philcox sent me a brilliant cartoon of exactly what I'd described, so I posted it on my website and was amazed by the response. Within twenty-four hours, I had dozens of visitors to the site from Morocco, Israel, Lebanon and pretty much every other olive oil producing country in the world. They'd presumably spotted "GM Self-Harvesting Olives" on Google or wherever and rushed eagerly to find out more. I can only imagine their disappointment when all they got was a cartoon of parachuting olives with miniature machetes and tiny little legs instead of a major new cost-cutting development in olive oil production. I even noticed on my website's statistical summary report for 2013 that the GM olives post was by far the most viewed of all the posts I'd done that year.

If you haven't seen the cartoon, you can find it on my website at www.rob-johnson.org.uk where you can also listen to the olive harvesting episode in its entirety. It's Episode Ten and it's called "I'd Rather Eat My Own Face", which should give you a bit of a clue how I feel about the annual bashing of our olive trees.

As a slight aside, it's quite interesting seeing which countries my website visitors come from and what they typed into a search engine to get there. Some of these are a bit odd, like "Samaras chickens", "dog with microphone", "comedy toilet images" and "Golden Dawn sinking" – nice thought – but my favourite so far has to be "string in stool sample". I can only hope that whoever put this into Google was someone who'd listened to my podcasts before and had a vague memory that the series was called *A Kilo of String* and that Episode Six included an item about how people setting up new food businesses in Greece have to provide a stool sample to the authorities because of some weird notion about health and safety. If not, then the person who was simply looking for information about "string in stool sample" must have had a serious health issue, and I sincerely hope they found some useful and encouraging advice on how to deal with it, but they certainly wouldn't have done from *my* website.

I did actually Google the phrase myself, and my website was the tenth item listed – with the rather unflattering title of "Stool samples – Rob Johnson". Fifth on the list was for wiki-answers.com with the title "What would cause white string-like things in your stool?" I didn't look up the answer to this, but I'd guess the article would be called something like "Eating white string", and the solution would be "Stop eating white string".

But back to my dread of the olive harvest and why I sometimes wonder if Vasilis had been right after all. Vasilis was – and probably still is – an architect/builder over on the Mani peninsula, which you may recall is where we rented a house when we first came to Greece. In fact, it was Vasilis who'd designed and built it – the house, that is, and not the Mani peninsula – and we'd been really impressed (although not nearly as impressed as we would have been if he *had* designed and built the Mani peninsula).

Anyway, he'd bought up several plots of land in the area and offered to show us a few of them with a view to building us a house on any one we liked. At the time, we still had open minds about where we wanted to live, so we accepted his invitation – although I didn't need much persuading once he'd mentioned buying us lunch during the tour.

Some of the places he showed us were certainly very tempting, but Penny and I were adamant that it would take somewhere pretty special to lure us away from Xerika, and we told Vasilis so over our free lunch.

'Kyparissia?' he said, almost choking on his calamari. 'Kyp-ar-iss-ia?' He repeated the name syllable by syllable with as much distaste as if we'd just told him we wanted to live next to a nuclear power station less than a kilometre downwind from a major sewage farm.

'Kyparissia, yes,' I said. 'Do you know it?'

'Know it? Of course I know it. The place is full of inbred idiot farmers who spend their days clogging up the roads with their clapped-out old tractors and only taking time out now and again when they feel like shagging a goat... or a donkey,' he added with heavy and portentous emphasis.

He was clearly not enamoured of the life agricultural nor Kyparissia in particular.

'Why you want to live in such a place? You want to break your backs growing olives the rest of your lives? – No, my friends, you buy one of my plots, I build you a beautiful house and a couple of holiday bungalows – more if you can afford it – and you sit back in the sun, sipping your ice cold beers by the pool and watch the money roll in.'

To be perfectly honest, there are times when I think back to Vasilis's words and wonder whether we should have followed his advice. These thoughts usually occur to me when I'm staring up into yet another olive tree, stretching to reach that last bunch of olives which are just out of range and cursing the pain which throbs through each elbow with every bash of my bashing stick. Sitting by a pool, sipping beer and watching the money roll in sounds pretty good by comparison.

183

I once read that, in ancient times, only virgins and young men sworn to chastity were allowed to harvest olive trees. Oh, if only I'd been an olive farmer in those days, I'd have had every excuse I could possibly have wished for.

ENDNOTE: By the way, for all those friends and relatives in Britain who've been promising for so long that they'd come out and help with our olive harvest some time and haven't yet made it – I'm just kidding. Honest. You'll love it!

26

I Can't Believe It's Not Butter

The olive oil we produce ourselves is fully certified as organic, and we've often been complimented on its quality. On the other hand, several of the local Greek farmers have repeatedly told us that we must be mad to grow our olives organically because we'd produce a lot more oil – and hence make a lot more money – if we followed their example and used the same kind of noxious chemicals which they regularly spray their trees with.

So entrenched is the non-organic method here that the olive presses impose a small levy on the oil you produce to pay the local authority to come and spray your trees for you. Being organic, we're exempt from paying this levy, but we still had to put up a big sign on our gate, saying "ORGANIC! NO SPRAYING!" – in Greek, of course.

Some of the people employed by the local authority to do the spraying can get a little over-zealous at times, which is hardly surprising since it's automatically assumed that everyone in the area wants their trees blasted with chemicals unless you give a clear indication to the contrary. Not long after we'd moved in to Xerika and before we'd put up our "NO SPRAYING!" sign, Penny woke up very early one morning when she heard a tractor on our land, and she rushed out of the house to see what was happening. By this time, the tractor was almost at the bottom of the land and its driver was already in the process of sorting out the spraying equipment.

'No spraying! Organic!' Penny kept shouting as she raced towards the tractor, flailing her arms and with her dressing gown flapping open as she ran.

Whether or not the tractor driver understood English or not, the very sight of this wild-haired crazy woman yelling at him and bearing down on him at speed was enough to stop him in his tracks, and he quickly packed away his spraying gear and trundled off out of the gate.

There are plenty of hoops to go through before you can be certified as organic in Greece, but probably no more than in the UK. The first thing we had to do was register with one of the two organic associations here, and we went with Bio-Hellas (the equivalent of the Soil Association in Britain), and each year, they send an inspector to check that we're not breaking any of the organic rules. Ours is called Elias, and although we've got to know him quite well over the years, his visits in the early days were a source of high anxiety. As soon as he arrived, he'd stroll around the land, periodically stopping to examine a tree and occasionally picking off a leaf and inspecting it minutely before tossing it to the ground and heading for another random tree.

All this time, Penny and I would trot along behind him, nervously expecting some critically damning remark at any moment. For those who are old enough to remember, it was very like one of those TV advertisements for Del Monte tinned fruit. Each one showed "The Man from Del Monte" (who was always dressed in a white suit and panama hat) wandering around some fruit orchard or other while a small group of poor peasants trailed along behind him, feverishly chewing their fingernails as they waited for him to give his verdict on whether the fruit was good enough for the

Del Monte label. Fortunately, the advert always ended with the white-suited man giving an approving nod and a smile and the voice-over announcing that 'The Man from Del Monte says "Yes"'. At this point, the peasants would breathe a huge sigh of relief and enthusiastically celebrate the fact that, for this year at least, they wouldn't all have to starve to death. (I sometimes wonder how often an advert ended up on the cutting room floor after The Man from Del Monte said "No".)

Once the inspection of the trees is completed to Elias's satisfaction, we then all sit down while he fills in his report and he asks us various questions such as, on one occasion, 'What sort of containers do you put your oil in when you sell it?'

'It depends,' I said. 'Sometimes five-litre cans and sometimes the sixteen- or seventeen-kilo cans.'

'They don't exist.'

'Pardon?'

'The sixteen- and seventeen-kilo cans. They don't exist.'

'Of course they do. There's at least four in our shed right now.'

Elias slowly put down his pen, leaned towards me across the table and narrowed his eyes at me as he very clearly enunciated the words: 'They. Don't. Exist.'

'So if they don't exist, how come there isn't a very big puddle of olive oil on the shed floor?'

'Okay, okay,' said Elias, sitting back again. 'We all know they actually *exist*. It's just that they're not supposed to. You're only allowed to sell olive oil in quantities no larger than five litres.'

(Incidentally, just to confuse matters further, and in keeping with the kilo of string theme, the bulk buying and selling of olive oil in Greece is done by the kilo, whereas smaller quantities – five litres and below – are bought and sold by the litre. No, I've no idea why, and in the case of olive oil there's really not much difference between the two measurements since a kilo of oil is equivalent to 1.1 litres.)

Another slightly surreal conversation we had with Elias, and also about olive oil containers, was when he told us that although the olive press we used was certified as organic for *pressing*, it wasn't certified for *bottling* the oil. Consequently, if we wanted to sell our oil as properly organic, we'd have to take the cans of oil we got from the press to a bottling plant that had organic certification.

'There's one a few kilometres from here on the road to Filiatra.'

'Okay,' I said. 'So let me get this straight. The press fills a load of cans with our oil, and then we take the cans to this bottling plant so they can pour it into some other cans, which are probably identical to the original ones, and only then can we sell it as fully organic.'

'Correct.'

Given such an emphatic response, there really didn't seem to be much point in challenging the logic of this, and as always in Greece, it's better to simply accept that this is the way it is and just get on with it.

As well as being fully organic, our oil is extra virgin, single estate and cold pressed, so it pretty much ticks all the boxes as far as quality is concerned. This is all well and good of course except for one thing... I have to confess that, personally speaking, I really don't like the stuff that much.

Okay, so it's well known that olive oil is incredibly healthy and helps to protect you from heart disease, high blood pressure, strokes, some forms of cancer and, for all I know, very possibly the Bubonic Plague and leprosy as well. So all in all, it's very good for you. Presumably, this means that as long as you deep fry things like chips in olive oil, this instantly turns them into a health food so you can eat as many as you like without feeling guilty. In Scotland, where they've tried deep frying in batter almost everything which is generally considered to be fit for human consumption – and maybe even some things that aren't – the Scots have gained a bit of a reputation for unhealthy eating. However, if they were to deep fry their pizzas, Mars bars and Cadbury's Cream Eggs in olive oil instead of whatever it is they use at the moment, this image would be transformed overnight. As yet, I haven't tried eating a Mars bar that's been deep fried in olive oil, but I'm sure if I did I'd feel as smug and self-righteous as if I'd just ploughed my way through a kilo of raw broccoli. Who knows? It may well even count as one of my "Five A Day".

But other than a way of convincing myself that anything deep fried in olive oil is good for you, I'm really not that fussed. All right, if you insist on using oil as a salad dressing, olive oil is definitely the best choice and is generally recommended by all of the top TV chefs. I certainly can't imagine the likes of Jamie Oliver saying: 'So I've literally finished putting together this literally bootiful salad, and literally all I need to do now is literally bosh some of this luvverly, golden, genetically modified sunflower oil all over it.' On balance, though, when it comes to salads, you can keep your olive oil vinaigrette as far as I'm concerned. Give me a big dollop of Hellman's mayonnaise any day of the week or even – at a pinch – a generous helping of good old-fashioned Heinz Salad Cream.

Greek people use olive oil by the barrel load, of course, because the whole country is awash with the stuff every winter after the olive harvest. In ancient times, they didn't just use it for cooking, they also used to daub themselves with it after a bath and wash their hair with it. I don't suppose many Greeks still use it for these purposes nowadays as there are plenty of alternatives on the market such as "Dr Papadopoulos's After Bath Embalming Gel" and "Shiny Locks Dandruff-Be-Gone All-In-One Shampoo, Conditioner and Scalp Scrub".

So what else do they use all this oil for? Well, for one, Greek people tend to use it instead of butter, which, for a country that pretty much invented the entire concept of civilisation, seems to me to be a retrograde step which almost borders on barbarism. I mean, I've never actually tried making a peanut butter or Marmite sandwich with olive oil instead of butter, but I imagine that the result must be pretty unpleasant to say the least. And what about toast? You sit down for your breakfast with a couple of slices, grilled to perfection, and then what? Whack on a load of olive oil and then a thick layer of Cooper's Old English chunky orange marmalade? I don't think so. Bring on the Lurpak, I say, and plenty of it.

It's just occurred to me that I've mentioned quite a few brand names in the last few paragraphs, so in the spirit of product placement, if anyone happens to be reading this book who works in the PR department of Cadbury's, Mars, Heinz, Hellman's, Marmite, Cooper's marmalade or Lurpak, please email me for details of where you can send all the free stuff. And if you're a manufacturer of genetically modified sunflower oil, please don't bother. By the way, did I say what a wonderful piece of machinery the Harley Davidson motorcycle is?

27

It's Just Not Cricket

Since Penny and I moved to Greece, we've often been asked what, if anything, we miss about Britain, and my answer is always much the same:

1. friends and family;
2. watching Crystal Palace play football;
3. a decent pint of beer (e.g. Fuller's London Pride or Chiswick) [FAO Fuller's Brewery: Please note product placement];
4. cricket.

This list isn't exhaustive or necessarily in order of importance, but I daren't say what the real order is for fear of upsetting the aforementioned friends and family. Having said that, we do manage to see most of our friends and family fairly regularly when they visit us here or when we're back in the UK. Likewise, I've managed to catch the occasional Crystal Palace game when we're in England and even been able to watch a few of their matches out here on the TV since they reached the heady heights of the Premier League.

Access to decent beer is a bit of a problem, although London Pride in tins can periodically be found in one of the bigger supermarkets in Kalamata (our nearest major city). The first time I came across it was a few years ago when we'd called in to do some food shopping, mainly for stuff we can't get locally such as Marmite and HP

191

Sauce. Penny and I were wandering separately around the shop when all of a sudden I heard her let out a shriek so loud that I thought she was having some kind of fit. Rushing over to her, I saw that she was standing in front of the canned beers section, her eyes wide and her mouth open as she pointed silently at the shelf bearing about two dozen cans of the liquid nectar commonly known as Fuller's London Pride.

'Amazing,' I said and leaned forward to check the price. 'Bit bloody expensive, though.'

'But that's in euros,' said Penny. 'It's not too bad if you convert it to pounds.' (NB: This was long before the post-Brexit plummeting of the pound against the euro.)

'Yeah, okay. I suppose I could get a few and just keep them for special occasions.'

With that, I picked up a pack of four cans, deposited them in the trolley and started to walk away.

'Four cans?' said Penny in a presumably unintentional homage to the Two Ronnies' classic *Four Candles* sketch. 'Is that it?'

I shrugged. 'Well, how many special occasions are we likely to have before these are past their sell-by date?'

I have to admit that I do have a marked tendency towards the "glass almost entirely empty" attitude to life, and never once have I clicked on the "I'm feeling lucky" option on Google. But in my defence, on the rare occasions when I do indulge myself in a flash of unrestrained optimism, this often results in something going horribly wrong. Maybe it's a character defect which derives from having been a Crystal Palace supporter since I was a kid because a Palace fan's default position is the expectation that failure is virtually inevitable.

The upside of this, though, is that whenever the club happens to notch up more than two victories on the trot or wins promotion to the Premier League or, as actually happened in 2016, makes it to the final of the FA Cup (only to be robbed of the trophy by a referee who obviously hadn't a clue how to apply the advantage rule), a Palace supporter's reaction is all the more ecstatic. But whether or not my lifelong support of Crystal Palace FC really is to blame, my generalised pessimism can sometimes irritate the hell out of Penny, and this was one such occasion.

'Look,' she said in a tone of voice which clearly signalled that any attempt at contradiction would be utterly futile, 'you've no idea if they'll ever have London Pride in again – maybe never – so you may as well make the most of it while you can.'

Even before she'd finished speaking, she began to pile cans of Fuller's finest into the trolley, and she didn't stop till the shelf was completely empty. Given the expense involved and the fact that Penny isn't a beer drinker herself, I must say how seriously impressed I was with this gesture of supreme selflessness, and it's very probably one of the many reasons I eventually asked her to marry me.

Moving on from the somewhat stereotypically British male's obsession with beer and football to the rather less commonly held belief that cricket is one of the finest sports ever invented, I'm sorry to say that Greece has been a major disappointment in this respect. I already knew before we moved here that basketball and football were by far the most popular sports in Greece and that the only place you could get to watch a game of cricket is on Corfu, primarily because the island has an inordinately high proportion of British expats who love nothing better than the glorious sound of leather on willow.

Undeterred, however, I carefully packed my precious Gray-Nicolls cricket bat and vowed there and then that I would not rest until the whole of Greece was awakened to the joys and delights of what, by rights, really ought to be called "the beautiful game". I would start small, of course, slowly building interest until there was a national Greek cricket team, which would rise slowly but surely up the world rankings to rival the likes of India and New Zealand.

That was the dream anyway, but thirteen years later I have to report that turning that dream into a reality hasn't been going terribly well. Hardly anyone in Greece has even *heard* of cricket, never mind actually watched a game, and whenever I've tried to describe it (often demonstrating with a mime of a mighty slog over mid-wicket for a certain six), the response is almost universally the same: 'Oh, you mean baseball' or occasionally: 'Oh, you mean golf'.

Truth be told, my dream of introducing cricket to Greece wasn't entirely altruistic as it would mean that I'd also have the opportunity to play myself. Not that I've ever been much good at it, but I do have all the gear – full whites, pads, stumps, bails and even a proper helmet complete with metal grille protection for the face. When I played cricket at school, protective helmets had not yet come into being, and the only protection the batsman had was a pair of pads and also gloves with rubber spiky bits which were supposedly designed to lessen the impact of a direct hit on the fingers and knuckles. Only a select few – those who played for the school teams – were issued with a "box", which, for the uninitiated, is a piece of hard, moulded plastic like a codpiece that covered the wearer's "gentleman's arrangements". It occurred to me at the time that this was highly elitist and the school's way of prioritising the preservation of only the best cricketers' genes in the gene pool.

The only opportunities I do get to play cricket myself nowadays are when British friends and relatives come to visit us. The games normally take place on the beach, mainly because it's almost impossible to find a substantial enough area of grass that isn't stuffed full of olive trees. Even though the wearing of full cricket whites is mostly dispensed with, our activities often generate a considerable amount of interest from the locals, most of whom appear to be utterly baffled as to what on earth we think we're doing. Once, a Greek guy in his early twenties came up to me after we'd finished playing for the day and asked me exactly that.

'Just now,' he said, half smiling and half frowning. 'What was it you were doing?'

'It's a game called cricket,' I said, sensing that he seemed genuinely interested and jumping at the chance to recruit the first Greek member of the Kyparissia Cricket Club.

With what I hoped was infectious enthusiasm, I launched into a brief explanation of the game, carefully avoiding the more complex aspects such as the LBW rule and the Duckworth-Lewis Method. I didn't want to confuse the guy after all, and as I went through the basics, he repeatedly nodded his understanding with what looked a lot like growing interest and approval. Growing, that is, until I reached the part about international matches.

'So, when one country plays another country, it's called a Test Match,' I said.

'Test Match,' he repeated with another nod of approval.

'Like Sri Lanka versus the West Indies or England against Australia,' I said, deliberately omitting any mention of The Ashes and how it got its name. 'And these matches go on for five days.'

This time, there was no nod of approval or even a flicker of understanding. On the contrary, the young guy's face froze instantly into an expression of bewildered disbelief and then, two seconds later, thawed into a beaming grin of the "Okay, you nearly had me going with that one" variety.

'One game lasts for five days?' he said.

'That's right, yes.'

'Five *days*?'

By now, he could barely contain his laughter, so I realised that further explanation was called for. 'Obviously, they don't play for the full twenty-four hours. They go away and sleep at night and then come back the next morning to start again. Then there's lunch, of course, and afternoon tea, and—'

But it was too late. The damage had already been done if the guy's peals of laughter were anything to go by. And they clearly were, because the next moment, he got to his feet, still chuckling, and patted me on the shoulder.

'Good joke,' he said and then wandered off up the beach, no doubt eager to tell his mates about the crazy English bloke and the even crazier game called "cricket".

My first potential recruit had been lost forever, and in the ensuing years, scarcely half a dozen non-Brits have shown the slightest interest in helping me to fulfil my dream – even though I no longer mention Test Matches at all. Of these half dozen, one is Romanian and the others Greek, and we only played three or four times before they all rebelled and began to play football instead. Not that it had been a particularly auspicious start to the Kyparissia Cricket Club despite having a decent sized area of grass to play our first practice game on. Mostly flat and totally devoid of olive trees, the land belonged to one of the Greek players, and he'd thoughtfully mown the grass the day before. But this was when the problems began. Soon after we'd started, one of the other Greek players – Yiorgos (who bears a striking resemblance to Georgie Best in his heyday) –

fell over when chasing after a ball and spent the next ten minutes sneezing his head off.

'I have the hay fever,' he said when the sneezing fit finally subsided enough for him to get a coherent sentence out. 'Maybe I shouldn't play any more.'

And he didn't. Yiorgos left the field that day, never to return. Or at least never to play cricket. As soon as the others had abandoned the cricket a couple of weeks later to play football instead, Yiorgos suddenly reappeared. Apparently, falling over on newly mown grass when playing football didn't affect his hay fever in the slightest.

On the more positive side, Kostas, whose land we played on, was seriously handy with the bat, which wasn't that surprising as he'd been educated at a school in England and was therefore the only one who'd actually played cricket before. What was more surprising was his bowling action, which involved hurling the ball as hard as he could from shoulder height to try and shatter the batsman's stumps. It was much like the action of a pitcher in a game of baseball, and no matter how many times I told him this was illegal under the rules of cricket, he refused to change his technique. It has to be said, though, that he did get some impressive results.

Then there was Theodoris, our Romanian player, who's also our local car mechanic. He'd never even heard of cricket before, but he's one of those people who always seems to jump at the chance to try anything new. Like Kostas, he was also pretty effective with the bat, although his technique was somewhat unorthodox at times. In fact, it wasn't so much unorthodox as totally bizarre. Whenever a ball was bowled to him that was a bit on the wide side – which happened fairly frequently – instead of leaving it, he'd launch himself sideways at full length, goalkeeper-like, with the bat in one hand as he tried to make contact. On each occasion, I'd remind him that he didn't have to risk serious injury as he'd get a run anyway when the ball was wide, but he'd just grin and do exactly the same thing the next time.

It was fun while it lasted, but when the entire "team" rebelled and switched to football, I was forced to admit defeat. If cricket is ever to become an established sport in Greece, it's going to take someone with a lot more tenacity and patience than I have. In the meantime, I'll have to settle for playing the occasional game on the beach with friends and family from the UK and listening to *Test Match Special* over the Internet. Still, hearing Henry Blofeld's vivid descriptions of pigeons landing on the pitch or a passing multi-coloured bus when there's a lull in the cricketing action definitely has its compensations.

28

Abnormal Service

Needless to say, cricket is never covered by any of the myriad television channels in Greece where football, basketball, volleyball and sometimes athletics are the most heavily featured sports. Ice-skating also seems to be quite popular, which is fine with Penny, but I remain to be convinced that prancing around in a skimpy and/or tight-fitting glitter-suit to a hideously distorted backing track can seriously be considered a sport. I don't care how many sequins the skaters have hand-sewn themselves, if ice-skating is a sport then so too is ballroom dancing, which is even less interesting to watch as hardly anyone ever falls over.

During the Winter Olympics, Greek TV almost always seems to prioritise ice-skating over every other sport except perhaps curling. I mean, what is this Greek obsession with ice? Maybe it has something to do with Greece being a hot country and the very act of staring at an ice rink for hours on end has a soothingly cooling effect on the viewer. But – and the clue's in the name – the Winter Olympics take place during the coldest months of the year here, so there has to be some other reason best known only to the programme schedulers themselves.

Whatever the reason, the more dramatic and exciting winter sports, such as the giant slalom skiing, snowboarding and bobsleigh, barely get a look-in. I happened to mention this when a small group of us had got together for an ouzo or two during the 2006 Turin Winter Olympics.

'I don't think I've seen more than five minutes of the bobsleigh the whole time the Games have been on,' said one of the assembled company, who shared my somewhat negative view of ice-skating.

'And what about the luge,' said another. 'My God, but you've got to have guts to do that.'

'Not as much as the skeleton,' said someone else. 'That's just insane.'

At this point in the discussion, a Scottish friend – who will remain anonymous for reasons that will become apparent – asked what the skeleton was as she'd never heard of it. Someone gave her a brief explanation, to which she replied, 'Oh, I'd quite like to see that. I've never seen anyone go down on a skeleton before.'

I seem to remember making some comment about not being an expert on the decomposition of the human body but that I very much doubted this was even a physical possibility.

Choosing to broadcast ice-skating instead of what I'd call "real sports" is just one of the many quirks of Greek television. For instance, although most of the channels seem to have got their acts together in the last few months or so, when we first moved to Greece we soon learned that TV listings were almost entirely hypothetical and rarely bore any relation to what was actually being broadcast. Times were completely arbitrary, and programmes invariably started considerably later than advertised – quite frequently by an hour or more. Not because there'd been some major breaking news story interrupting the earlier programmes but simply because... Well, I've no idea why, other than to assume that this is just another example of the relaxed, sigá-sigá attitude to life which is so deeply entrenched in

200

the Greek character.

The general lack of urgency in the Greek way of life is, as I've mentioned before, one of the many positive aspects of living here, although every so often it can be somewhat irritating. Appointments are almost unheard of in Greece, and even if you *are* given a time to show up for your eye test, dental checkup or whatever, this is entirely notional, and you'll usually have to sit around in the waiting room – sometimes for a couple of hours – until your turn comes round. Similarly with the TV listings, there's no point setting up to record your favourite programme while you're out unless your device has one of those handy little gadgets for only starting to record when the programme actually begins. Otherwise, you'll more than likely end up with an hour and a half of some nonsense that you wouldn't watch even if your life depended on it – like ice-skating, for instance.

Something else which we had to get used to during our early days in Greece, but which has also been improved in more recent times, are the commercial breaks. I should emphasise here that I don't mean the advertisements themselves have got any better but only the way in which the breaks are scheduled. Back then, the TV stations appeared to pay little or no attention to what might be a suitable moment to interrupt a programme. The film, or whatever you were watching, would abruptly stop and the adverts would begin, very often in the middle of a conversation between characters and sometimes in the middle of a sentence. At the precise moment when Hercule Poirot says, 'And the name of the murderer is—', you'd suddenly go straight into an advert for some brand of shampoo or washing powder and have to wait patiently through a load more ads before you could find out who dunnit. I can only assume that the commercial breaks were set to begin according to some kind of automatic timer or that the advertiser had stipulated a specific time for their ad to be shown, regardless of where it came during the programme.

Nor was there ever any warning. No TV station jingle or logo, just straight into the adverts. One of the first things Penny and I watched on Greek television was the movie, *Airplane 2*, and there's a point in the film where the Ted Striker character looks through the cockpit window of the plane and says, 'I think we're seriously off course.' The very next shot was an image of the Milky Way, which did at least make some kind of sense in the context until we realised it was the beginning of an advertisement.

The length of the commercial breaks is also a source of some irritation, and this is something which *hasn't* improved over the years. During the course of a single film, each break can last anything from three to fifteen minutes or more, and you never know which it's going to be. According to Sod's Law, it's almost always at the start of one of the short breaks that you decide you've got plenty of time to get the washing-up done, but you've only just filled the bowl with water when the programme starts again.

One thing you can be fairly confident of, however, is that there'll be a commercial break of ten to fifteen minutes less than five minutes before the end of the film. Even though you're pretty sure that all that remains is the inevitable final scene where the two main characters hug and kiss while they congratulate each other on saving the planet from almost certain destruction, you still have to sit through the ads in case the climax isn't as predictable as you'd expected. Usually, it is, so that's another fifteen minutes of your life you'll never get back – unless of course you've guessed correctly for once and managed to use the time to get the washing-up done.

Producing programmes as cheaply as possible is of course a priority for most TV stations these days, never mind which country they're broadcasting in, and Greece is no exception. One of its latest offerings is a "light entertainment" show called *Rantevoú* (Rendezvous), and it's almost identical to the UK's *Blind Date*, which was hosted by Cilla Black and ran from 1985 to 2003. But the only reason I mention this programme at all is because of the title as it appears at the beginning of the show. Given the differences between the Greek and Latin alphabets, and especially upper case letters, *Rantevoú* is written in Greek capitals as "PANTEBOY", which strikes me as rather inappropriate for a programme about dating – or maybe not.

Another show which one of the Greek channels tried to do on the cheap was *Who Wants to be a Millionaire?* Somewhat bizarrely, even though the show followed *exactly* the same format as the original and kept the same title, the most a contestant could win was €150,000. It wouldn't have made much more sense if Greece had still been using the drachma because even a top prize of a million drachma would have made the show the equivalent of *Who Wants to Win Five Quid?* – 'Right, your seventy-five pence is safe, so you might as well play the next question.'

Quite apart from the comparatively miserly prize money, the Greek version of the show was almost totally lacking in the kind of drama we'd come to expect from *WWTBAM?* in the UK. Once again, this seemed to be yet another manifestation of the generally laid-back attitude of most Greeks and, apparently, the majority of the contestants were similarly inclined. Despite the familiar, tension-building jingles and the host of the show's best efforts to ramp up the suspense, the result was usually much the same:

HOST:	Just to make sure you're clear about this, Yanni, I have to remind you that if you answer this question incorrectly, you'll lose the €1,500 you already have.
CONTESTANT:	Yeah, okay.
HOST:	So take your time and—
CONTESTANT:	B.
HOST:	I'm sorry?
CONTESTANT:	B. The answer is B.
HOST:	You're sure about that, are you?
CONTESTANT:	(with a shrug) Not really, no.
HOST:	Perhaps you should spend a bit more time to—
CONTESTANT:	D.
HOST:	What?
CONTESTANT:	I've changed my mind. It's D.
HOST:	(failing to stifle a sigh) You realise that if you're wrong, you'll lose €1,500?
CONTESTANT:	Yep.
HOST:	Perhaps you should consider sticking with the money you've already won and—
CONTESTANT:	D.
HOST:	D?
CONTESTANT:	Yep.
HOST:	And is that your final answer?
CONTESTANT:	Yep. D.
HOST:	Very well then, let's see if you've doubled your money and won €3,000 or if you've lost €1,500.

(Cue dramatic music for several seconds until "A" lights up as the correct answer.)

HOST:	I'm sorry, Yanni, but I'm afraid you've just *lost* €1,500.
CONTESTANT:	(with another shrug) Oh well, never mind.

To be fair, when Penny and I first watched the Greek version of *WWTBAM?*, it was several years before the economic crisis, so contestants might be much more cautious nowadays about losing what for many people would be a substantial boost to their income. But this we'll never know because the show was axed in 2006. I wonder why.

Something else – or rather, some*one* else – that was axed a few years ago was the weather forecaster on Star TV, one of Greece's many privately owned television stations. Petroula, as she was called, appeared on our screens every evening wearing a low cut and abundantly filled top and informed us what tomorrow's weather would be in a voice that seemed to be a deliberate imitation of Marilyn Monroe "singing" to President Kennedy at his forty-fifth birthday bash. Petroula's provocative gyrations were brought to an abrupt halt, however, when Greece's state broadcasting watchdog (ESR) suddenly decided that she was "harming the quality of programming and insulting human dignity". I'm not sure why it took the ESR more than twelve months to reach this conclusion, although I doubt that it had much to do with the usual rationale of *sigá-sigá*.

But the Star TV channel was determined not to return to the pre-Petroula days of weather forecasting, so instead of Petroula, we then had a youngish guy in a dark suit, thin black tie and sunglasses with more than a passing resemblance to punk poet, John Cooper Clarke. Hardly very revolutionary in itself, of course, except that the whole of each forecast was performed as a rap. Something like this (but in Greek):

> Will it rain or will it snow?
> That's the stuff you wanna know,
> So listen up,
> I'll take it slow.
> Ain't no need for heavy coats
> Or woolly hats they make from goats.
> Ain't gonna rain and ain't gonna snow
> And no degrees below zero.
> Instead o' that, the sun'll shine
> And temps'll get to twenty-nine.
> So chill it out and keep your cool
> 'Cos I know the truth. I ain't no fool.

It's probably very clear from the above that I'm not a big fan of rap music and therefore don't have much idea how to write it, although I do respect the amount of effort that must have gone into producing a different rap every day to forecast the weather. I was even a little disappointed when, like Petroula, Yannis Cooper Clarkopoulos (or whatever his name was) vanished from our screens. Perhaps the ESR felt that rap music was also "insulting human dignity" – and there'd be many who wouldn't disagree – but I suspect the rapping guy was simply a victim of budget cuts because, since then, Star TV's weather forecasts have consisted solely of a map of Greece with the usual symbols and a voice-over commentary.

As a Brit, it's obviously etched into my very soul that the weather is an extremely serious subject, so I'd be forced to agree with the ESR's rather dim view of meteorologically irreverent antics. On the other hand, I've found the ESR's stance on other broadcasting issues to be entirely devoid of logic. The categorisation of individual programmes (e.g. whether they're suitable for children to watch) often appears to have been decided completely at random. Although this probably isn't exclusively the fault of the ESR, and individual TV stations must take much of the responsibility, programmes which contain pretty raunchy sex scenes are frequently aired without any warnings at all, and the so-called "watershed" is virtually non-existent. Conversely, I've seen episodes of dramas such as *Silent Witness* quite late at night where the cadaver on the pathologist's slab is pixelated from head to toe. So, it's absolutely fine for kids to watch full-on, full-frontal sex scenes, but apparently even adults mustn't be allowed to see a naked corpse, despite the fact that it's probably a dummy and not even a real human body.

Finally, to conclude this mini-critique of the vagaries of Greek television, I must at least mention the sometimes bizarre subtitling of English language programmes. I understand, of course, that literal translations are not always possible or even desirable, but what earthly reason could there be for translating the line, "I'll meet you at six o'clock" as *"tha sas synantíso se pénte i óra"* (I'll meet you at *five* o'clock)? Clearly, it has nothing to do with the time difference between Greece and Britain, which is two hours and not one, so why the change? Fair enough that miles and yards are translated into their metric equivalents, but six o'clock is surely six o'clock in anybody's language and has nothing to do with different systems of measurement.

Even so, this kind of mistranslation of specific details happens fairly often and isn't always confined to times of the day. For instance, "I'm thirty-four years old" can become any number between thirty and forty years old, and a serial killer's victims can sometimes be increased or decreased entirely at the whim of the subtitler. Not having seen the film on Greek TV, I've no idea whether there are eighty-nine dalmatians or a hundred and twelve, but I'm looking forward to watching *The Magnificent Nine* and *Two Weddings and Three Funerals*.

I'm a hundred per cent certain, though, that the Greek subtitlers are never going to mess with *300*, which, for those who don't know the film already, is about a small army of three hundred Spartan warriors who heroically defended the invasion of Greece by three hundred thousand Persians. Well, I say I'm a hundred per cent certain, but if this book ever gets translated into Greek, I'll probably only be ninety per cent certain.

29

For a Few Euros More

Greek television has usually been slow to catch on to the latest technological developments, but something it did embrace with open arms was the ability to split the screen into several separate sections. But unlike most kids who've been given a new toy to play with, the novelty has never worn off. On the contrary, in all the years that Penny and I have lived in Greece, I don't recall watching a single news or current affairs programme which didn't use the split screen format for at least some, if not all, of its airtime. Quite often, the producer seems to have got rather carried away and has had as many as ten little boxes on the screen at the same time, each with a talking head inside it – or a head that's waiting to talk. Generally, these heads belong to politicians, journalists or so-called experts on the matter being discussed.

This is all very well unless you happen to have a portable TV set with a very small screen, as we did when we first moved here. Any more than six boxes means that each one appears at about the size of a large postage stamp. Not only that – and this obviously isn't the fault of the split screen technology itself – but often half or more of the talking heads aren't so much talking as shouting, and all at the same time. With each trying to out-shout the others, I defy even a native Greek speaker to understand more than the occasional snippet of what they're banging on about.

The more patient of the contributors, who are usually reporters on an outside broadcast linkup, sometimes have to wait ten minutes or more before they're called upon to speak. Almost inevitably, some of them seem to forget that they're on camera at all, and I've seen various manifestations of sheer boredom, including one such reporter scratching his scalp and then closely examining his fingernails to check the results.

As even the least observant reader will have noticed by now, I have, if I say so myself, rather neatly segued from a chapter on television to a chapter on politics. No book on Greece would be complete without one, of course, and not only because of the economic crisis which has plagued the country in recent years, but also because it's a subject that most Greeks are intensely interested in.

Politics and current affairs rank very highly here as favourite topics of conversation, much like football, soap operas and the weather do in the UK, and one place you're almost guaranteed to hear a spontaneous political debate is the *kafeneío*. These are no-frills-whatsoever cafés, which in the past have been the exclusive preserve of men, most of whom are approaching or beyond retirement age. Nowadays, however, the clientele of most *kafeneía* is far more mixed in terms of both gender and age, but their reputation as "little parliaments" still remains steadfastly intact.

It is quite possibly *because* the Greeks are more politically aware than the majority of Brits that they also tend to be considerably more forthright in expressing their contempt for politicians in general. This distrust of politicians – hatred even – is so ingrained in the Greek character that I always get exactly the same response whenever (almost every 5th November) I explain about Guy Fawkes and how the British burn him in effigy: 'I don't understand. Why would you celebrate that he *failed* to blow up the Houses of Parliament?'

Such an attitude is hardly surprising for the simple reason that the economic crisis in Greece and the country's subsequent plunge into the abyss of austerity were largely the result of decades of political mismanagement and corruption. This in turn has resulted in Greece's reputation for rampant tax evasion. Since ordinary Greek citizens are fully aware that a large chunk of taxpayers' money ends up in various back pockets rather than being spent on schools, hospitals, public services, etcetera, they simply don't trust the state to spend tax revenues on what it's supposed to spend them on. Wherever possible, therefore, the majority of transactions are carried out in cash to avoid the necessity for any paperwork which the tax authority might find of interest. Consequently, among its many conditions for lending Greece money, the triumvirate of the European Commission, European Central Bank and the International Monetary Fund has insisted on a range of tax reforms which are supposedly designed to overcome the problem of tax evasion.

One such brilliant idea has been to tax people on what is called "deemed income", which essentially means that the tax authority guesses what you earn based on such things as the size of your house and your car. So, for instance, a single person is assumed to earn 3,000 euros a year just to survive, and if they live in a house of up to sixty square metres and they've got a 1200cc car, that's another 6,400 euros a year. Subtract the five grand tax threshold, and he or she will have to pay 22% tax on 4,400 euros – that's almost 1,000 euros. Fair enough if you've actually earned the kind of money the state guesses you have, but there's an awful lot of unemployed people in Greece now whose income is nowhere near what's imputed. But apparently, that's just tough. They'll have to pay the tax anyway, but where they'll find the money is another matter altogether.

If you also happen to own a small boat, then that's another 6,000 in deemed income – or an extra 1,320 euros in tax that you'll have to pay. Here's what might happen when a Greek tax inspector calls someone in to go over their tax return:

INSPECTOR: You do realise you could be fined for failing to declare your ownership of a boat?

TAXPAYER: But it's my kid's inflatable dinghy. It's bright yellow and got pictures of Mickey Mouse all over it.

INSPECTOR: Does it float?

TAXPAYER: Of course it floats. It wouldn't be much use if—

INSPECTOR: Then it's a boat. Which means you have an extra deemed income of 6,000 euros a year.

TAXPAYER: For a kid's toy? Huh, next thing you'll be charging me for his inflatable dolphin.

INSPECTOR: (leafing through papers) It seems you haven't declared that either.

TAXPAYER: Oh for—

As I mentioned above, the justification for taxing people on their deemed income is that it's supposed to be a way of tackling tax evasion, and although most people would agree that this is certainly something Greece needs to get on top of, it's hardly the fairest way of going about it. I suspect it's yet another case of the state taking the easiest option since guessing what people earn is much less time-consuming than trying to keep tabs on what people really earn and all the bothersome paperwork that goes with it.

Meanwhile, there are plenty of wealthy Greeks who have managed to evade paying any taxes at all on huge sums of very real income, much of which they have secretly stashed away in Swiss bank accounts. As far back as 2010, a list of more than two thousand of these "alleged" tax evaders – including a fair few politicians – was given to the then Greek government by Christine Lagarde, who was France's Finance Minister at the time and is the current head of the IMF. The intention was to help Greece crack down on its endemic tax evasion, but seven years later, hardly anyone on the so-called "Lagarde List" has been brought to justice and ordered to pay the tax that they owe.

Given that the people on the list have friends in high places or are in high places themselves, this isn't exactly a big surprise. Indeed, the very existence of the list was only made known to the public in 2012, with various politicians and civil servants denying that they'd ever even seen it and others saying they'd seen it but then lost it. Something along the lines of:

'You seen that list, Antoni?'

'Er, what list would that be then?'

'The one with the names of a load of Greeks with Swiss bank accounts. On a CD. You know the one. That French woman gave it us.'

'What, the woman with the white hair and the fake orange Tango tan?'

'That's the one, yeah. What's her name? Er…'

'Christine Lagarde. Yeah, I remember now.'

'So what happened to the CD then?'

'Poh, dunno, mate. Got an idea the Finance Minister's using it as a bird scarer down on his allotment.'

Or something like that anyway.

The list having finally been located, the editor of an independent Greek magazine, *Hot Doc*, published the names in a special edition and was immediately arrested for "breaching privacy laws". Two years in which the government and its officials had done absolutely nothing to investigate two thousand potential tax evaders and about two hours to arrest the guy who dared to make their names public. Fortunately, some form of justice prevailed and Kostas Vaxevanis, the editor in question, was almost immediately acquitted when his case came to trial.

On a more positive note, Greece has had some success in tackling tax evasion, however, as the driver of a bakery lorry was fined and stripped of his driving licence a couple of years ago for transporting – wait for it – four cheese pies which didn't have the necessary receipts or other documentation. That's right. Forget all the fat cats and corrupt politicians with billions hidden away in Swiss bank accounts, but beware of Greeks bearing undocumented cheese pies.

30

Who Dares, Cuts Hair

As well as clamping down on tax evasion, the Greek government has reduced its expenditure by the introduction of a range of austerity measures, mostly at the insistence of the European Commission, the European Central Bank and the International Monetary Fund. This has resulted in massive unemployment and drastic cuts in pensions and the wages of those who are fortunate enough to still be in a job. There are, however, many other savings the government could make which would have a much less damaging impact on the Greek people.

For instance, the cost of holding elections seems to be ludicrously expensive if the local authority ones are anything to go by. We've voted in a few of these now as only Greek citizens are allowed to vote in national elections, and one thing that's struck me every time we go to our village polling station is the ridiculous amount of wasted paper. There's one five-and-a-half-inch wide sheet of paper for each party that's standing, and several of these sheets are nearly two feet long, depending on the number of the party's candidates. (That's fourteen by sixty centimetres if you want to be metric about it.)

At our last local election, there were no less than forty-three of these sheets, and each voter is given the whole batch from which to make their selection. You then go into one of the booths and mark your crosses next to your five or six preferred candidates – but you can't vote for more than one party, so only one sheet of paper gets used. The rest normally get left in the booth or end up on the floor, which, according to my calculations amounts to 38.5 square feet (3.6 square metres) of wasted paper per voter.

Once you've made your selections, you fold your ballot paper and then wrap it in a blank piece of paper before putting it into an envelope – and not just any old bog standard office-supply manila job either. These envelopes are the quality, pale blue, self-sealing Basildon Bond types that posh people used to put their letters in when letter-writing was still deemed to be a valid form of communication.

The whole process must cost a fortune in stationery alone, not to mention a recycling headache of mammoth proportions – always assuming that all this waste paper does get recycled of course. And what about the poor tellers? How much more time does it take opening all those fancy envelopes and removing the blank sheet of paper even before you get to actually start counting the votes?

I mean, I know that ballots are supposed to be secret, but how much more secretive could you get, short of sticking your voting slip in a safety deposit box in some bank vault or other with the instruction: "Only to be opened in the event of my death"? Still, the Greeks pretty much invented democracy, so I suppose they know what they're doing.

One area where the Greek government has successfully managed to reduce its expenditure – and one of its few belt-tightening measures that it's difficult to fault – is the reduction in the number of jobs that were previously classed as "hazardous". Until fairly recently, there were as many as five hundred and eighty job categories in Greece which were considered sufficiently hazardous to merit early retirement on a full state pension (at the age of fifty for women and fifty-five for men). Not at all unreasonably, this applied to coal miners and those involved in bomb disposal, for instance, but hairdressers? Apparently, these heroic practitioners of the tonsorial art were allowed to retire early because they are exposed to "dangerous chemicals" on an almost daily basis. But then there's radio and TV presenters, who could take their pensions early because of all the germs lurking on their microphones. Wind instrument musicians were also entitled to hang up their bassoons and oboes well before the normal retirement age because they're prone to gastric reflux from all the puffing and blowing they do.

I swear I'm not making this up, and surely if you looked hard enough, you'd be able to make a case for every single job on the planet having some kind of potentially hazardous element to it. At the very least, you're going to be exposed to a whole range of unpleasant and possibly life-threatening bacteria unless you happen to work in a hermetically sealed environment without any human or animal contact, but I can't think of any job that applies to except perhaps writing. But even then, what about repetitive strain injury from all that typing and the detrimental effects on the eyes from staring at a (sometimes blank) computer screen all day long? Then of course there's the endless stream of cigarettes and coffee which is obviously indispensable to the work of any writer. Or is that just me?

Since the beginning of Greece's economic crisis, however, the state has been gradually reforming the country's pension laws – with some less-than-gentle encouragement from Europe and the IMF – and the list of hazardous occupations has been drastically reduced. Radio presenters, trombonists and the thousands of others who'll now have to continue working into their sixties weren't very happy of course, and if I was the Greek minister responsible for introducing the hazardous job reforms, I'd certainly be avoiding a trip to the hairdresser any time soon.

In addition to reducing the number of occupations on the hazardous jobs list, another way in which the Greek government has sought to reduce its outgoings was to check out whether the enormous number of people claiming disability benefits really were disabled. It isn't of course unreasonable for any government to attempt to save money by cutting benefits to fraudulent claimants, although the *British* government has clearly decided that even more money can be saved by cutting benefits to those who are genuinely in need of financial support. The new eligibility requirements it has introduced will have devastating consequences for the 160,000 *bona fide* claimants who will have their benefit payments severely reduced or axed altogether, and 50,000 disabled people have already had their specially adapted cars and other vehicles taken from them.

But that's another story, and hopefully the Greek government has no intention of adopting such draconian measures – unless, of course, the EU and the IMF decide to add these to their ever expanding list of bailout conditions. For the time being at least, Greece has probably got enough on its hands investigating the potentially fraudulent claims.

The government's suspicions were perhaps first aroused when it discovered that there was an unusually high number of people claiming benefits for leprosy and amputations in some parts of the country, and on the island of Zakynthos there were seven hundred registered blind out of a population of less than forty thousand. That's about 1.8% – nine times the prevalence of blindness in European countries according to a 2004

World Health Organisation study. Oh yes, and one of the blind people of Zakynthos was found to be a working taxi driver, and another was described as a bird hunter. Is that actually a job?

Part of the government's strategy for finding out who was legitimately entitled to disability benefits and who wasn't was to ask all of the country's claimants to re-register in person. This turned out to be quite an effective ploy as only a hundred of Zakynthos's seven hundred registered blind people actually turned up.

Of these, only forty were found to be genuinely blind, which rather begs the question: Why did the fraudulent sixty even bother? Did they all arrive wearing dark glasses, brandishing white sticks and bumping into furniture when they came into the office? And how did they get found out? Perhaps when the official had finished filling in the form for each claimant, they passed it to them and asked them to sign it, then waited to see which ones said, 'What, here on this dotted line? ... Oh damn, you got me bang to rights.' Or maybe the official dropped a fifty euro note on the floor, and whoever picked it up was obviously dodgy.

Not quite so dodgy – in fact, something which has been totally legitimate for decades – is that the unmarried daughters of dead civil servants and military personnel have been able to receive their deceased parent's pension for the duration of their own lifetimes, regardless of whether or not they were in employment themselves. In 2013, when the Greek government reduced these payments or axed them altogether, there were about 35,000 women who were getting as much as 1,000 euros a month just because they weren't married and their dads or mums happened to have worked for the civil service or the military before they died. In one case, a woman had been getting a monthly pension of 318 euros ever since her army officer father died in 1945, and who could blame her for choosing to stay single for all that time? I'm sure there are plenty of people who'd be glad to forego wedded bliss for a quarter of a million euros.

31

Wedding Bells
and Chicken Livers

Quarter of a million euros to forego "wedded bliss" certainly wasn't the reason why Penny and I almost decided against getting married. It was all the hoops to be jumped through – British as well as Greek ones – that made us seriously question whether tying the knot was going to be worth all the bother.

It all began in the early evening of 31st December 2013. We were just about to go out to a New Year's Eve party when, somewhat spontaneously, we decided to get married. (There were some practical reasons for reaching this decision, although I shan't mention them here for fear of detracting from the romance of the occasion.) Neither of us being particularly traditionalist, I was quite surprised when Penny insisted I should go down on one knee to propose, but I duly obliged – three times. My first attempt was rejected with the words, 'I'm not accepting a proposal while you're giggling', and the second with, 'I'm not accepting a proposal in a Donald Duck voice', but I finally got it right on the third time of asking.

I should point out here – but only because Penny told me I must – that when she accepted my proposal, I immediately did what she's subsequently described to all and sundry as "a happy dance". As far as I can recall,

I've never done a happy dance in my life, and I'm not even sure I'd know how to do one in the unlikely event that I ever felt the urge. And on this occasion, any physical gyrations on my part were entirely due to the sudden awareness that a mosquito had somehow found its way inside my underpants while I happened to be doing the washing-up.

But happy dance or not, and despite a couple of false starts, proposing marriage turned out to be the easiest part of the process by far. What followed was a bureaucratic nightmare of hair-tearing-out-by-the-handful proportions, and to cut an absurdly long and convoluted story short, here are just some of the stages we had to go through before the wedding could take place:

1. Go to British Embassy in Athens armed with birth certificates and all sorts of other official documents to get Certificate of Non-Impediment, which is basically confirmation that we weren't already married to someone else.

2. Pay British Embassy a shedload of cash for certificate and then find out that Greek authorities won't accept birth certificates, etcetera, unless they've been issued within the past six months.

3. Contact local authorities in UK to request re-issue of certificates. 'Why? Have you lost the originals?' – 'No, but the Greek authorities won't accept the originals.' – 'Ah yes, Greece. I see.'

4. Get re-issued certificates sent to the Foreign and Commonwealth Office in Milton Keynes to have something called an Apostille stamp added to them to prove they're the genuine

articles.

5. Have the Apostille-stamped certificates sent to Greece and then forwarded to the Greek Foreign Office in Athens to have them officially translated into Greek.

6. Take the whole lot to our local *Dimarcheío* (Town Hall) to make formal request for a registry office wedding.

7. Conduct absurd conversation with the woman in charge who peruses all the documents and then says, 'This Certificate of Non-Impediment is in Greek. Where's the English version?'
'There isn't one.'
'Why not?'
'Because you only asked for it in Greek, so the British Embassy only issued it in Greek.'

This was true. We'd first been to the Town Hall five months previously to find out what papers we needed to get married, and this same woman had given us a long list, but nowhere on that list did it say anything about the Cert of Non-Imp being in any language other than Greek. Not only that, but since this woman didn't speak a word of English, we'd no idea why she'd *want* an English version. Eventually, she acquiesced and moved on to a detailed examination of Penny's birth certificate – the version in English.

'What's this?' she said, pointing to the handwritten text in the column headed "Father's Occupation".

'It's my father's occupation,' said Penny. 'Schoolmaster. It's an older way of saying "teacher"?'

'Your father's name is Schoolmaster?'

'No. John.'

'John Schoolmaster?'

It was at this point that we referred her to the attached

Greek translation of Penny's birth certificate, which she'd asked for in her original list and which we'd paid quite a lot of money for. This seemed to satisfy her, but she then started a lengthy interrogation about why Penny's current surname (Phillips) wasn't the same as her maiden name (Wallbridge). We explained that Penny had kept the surname from her previous marriage, but this seemed to cause the woman a mild heart attack. She told us that, under Greek law, divorced women must revert to their maiden names so we couldn't get married unless Penny changed her name on all her official documents, including passport, Greek residence permit, driving licence and all the rest of it.

Suddenly, the idea of wedded bliss began to lose its appeal, but once again we managed to persuade her that her demands were not only unreasonable but also entirely unnecessary. After a few more hoops and a phone call to Athens (possibly the Ministry for Nonsensical Bureaucracy), she finally accepted that all our papers were in order, got us to sign the application form and put the date of our wedding in the official diary.

Since this was only a matter of days away, we'd begun to wonder until that moment whether the wedding would be able to go ahead at all. This would have been seriously annoying, but mostly for the several friends and relatives who'd made the effort to come over from the UK and Ireland especially for the occasion. All was well in the end, though, and despite the numerous bureaucratic hurdles we'd had to overcome, Penny and I had a really great day.

As we'd intended, it was a fairly low-key affair, and we didn't go out of our way to observe many of the British or Greek traditions which are normally associated with such an event. One particular Greek tradition which we were both heartily glad to avoid – but one which, for reasons that will become apparent, hardly ever happens these days – was told to us by a Greek friend, Kostas, about his grandmother's wedding. When she got married, it was the norm in those days for the newlyweds' immediate families to assemble on the morning after the first wedding night to inspect the undersheet from the marital bed. This was so they could check for themselves that the bride had still been a virgin prior to the marriage, but as Kostas's grandmother had said to him with a wink and a grin, 'It's amazing what you can do with a couple of chicken livers.'

And here's another Greek wedding-related story which, although it was told to me as a joke, I suspect has more than a ring of truth about it:

A young Greek guy called Sotiris tells his mother that he's asked a woman to marry him and she's accepted.

'But just for fun,' he says, 'I'll bring three women here tomorrow evening and you have to guess which one I've asked to be my wife.'

So the next day, he brings three women and they sit side by side on the settee while they spend the evening chatting with the mother. After they've gone, Sotiris asks his mother which one she thinks he's asked to marry him.

'The one in the middle,' says his mother without a moment's hesitation.

'But that's amazing. You're right, but how did you know?'

'I don't like her,' says the mother.

This might also explain why Greek men generally tend to marry a little later in life than the average Brit, often living with their parents until their early to mid thirties before flying the nest. In fact, as I've been told on many occasions, this is one of the justifications for claiming that Jesus must have been Greek: 'Like Jesus, most Greek men live with their parents until they're in their mid thirties, do the same jobs as their fathers, and their mothers think they're God.'

What makes this joke less funny than it used to be, however, is that so many Greeks have now been forced to return once again to live under their parents' roofs, often with children of their own. This is a direct consequence of the austerity measures that have been imposed since the beginning of the economic crisis, which have resulted in massive unemployment and drastic wage cuts. Unable to afford the rent or mortgage repayments on their own flats and houses any longer, many Greek people have had little option but to throw themselves on their parents' mercy. It is not at all uncommon, therefore, that three generations of a family now live in one apartment with the only income provided by the grandparents' pensions, which have themselves been axed by as much as 40%. According to a survey carried out towards the end of 2016, 49.2% of all Greek households were having to live on the pension of one family member.

There's an old Greek proverb which translates as: "He who suffers much will know much". If that's the case, then there must be an awful lot of Greeks who have become incredibly wise since the beginning of the economic crisis.

32

Last Impressions

It's no good crying over lavishly spilt falsehoods and disinformation, of course, but I believe that Britain's decision to leave the EU will go down in history as one of the biggest and gravest mistakes the British voting public has ever made. Even in the immediate aftermath of the referendum result, the disturbingly negative impacts were already plain for all to see. Not only have there been serious financial consequences, such as the pound plummeting in value, but also an alarming upsurge in overt racism of the "foreigners go home" variety.

Several people have asked us how we'll be affected as non-EU citizens living in an EU country, but the honest answer is: 'We've absolutely no idea.' But nor does anyone else – including the British government – until negotiations with the EU have been completed, and that could take anything up to two years. One thing is certain, however, and that is that Penny and I have no intention of leaving Greece unless the government decides to kick us out, which I think is highly unlikely.

Back in 2012, when yet another round of stringent austerity measures were introduced by the Greek government as part of its bailout deal with the EU, some of the public demonstrations turned to riots, and William Hague, the British Foreign Secretary at the time, even issued a warning to all Brits in Greece that they should register with the British Embassy in case they had to be evacuated. Perhaps he'd seen *The Killing Fields* a few times too many, but the situation really wasn't that bad, and we never did bother to register with the Embassy to book our places on the first RAF transport plane out of here.

But partly because of Hague's ill-advised and inflammatory remarks, friends and relatives in the UK asked us a similar "How will it affect you?" kind of question that they've been asking us recently in the wake of the EU referendum. More specifically, they wanted to know if we'd leave Greece and come back to live in Britain, and our answer was much the same then as it is now, and the only reasons we would have repatriated ourselves were if there'd been a military coup or the neo-Nazi *Chrysí Avgí* (Golden Dawn) party had taken over the government. As yet, neither of these horror scenarios has come into being, so we're still here and happy to be so.

Another reason why friends and family in the UK have been worried about our wellbeing stems from the way in which the British media has reported on the situation in Greece. Ever since the beginning of the economic crisis here, the non-Greek media has generally painted a pretty damning – and damaging – picture of the country and portrayed most of its population as workshy, ouzo-guzzling tax dodgers who inspire jokes like: "How many Greeks does it take to change a light bulb? – None. They get an Albanian to do it". I can't deny that there are a fair few of these people in Greece, but probably no more so than in Britain or any other country. In the UK, we're just a bit more subtle about our schemes for making as much money as possible for as little work as we can get away with. It's the same in many countries, I'm sure, but the British also consider tax avoidance to be perfectly acceptable, whereas tax evasion is very very naughty indeed. To my mind, they both amount to the same thing – cheating the taxman – or tax person to be strictly politically correct.

Tax evasion has certainly been rife in Greece for decades, and according to the Greek Finance Ministry's figures in 2011, the state was owed a little over forty-one billion euros in unpaid taxes. However, the statistic I find particularly interesting is that eighty-five per cent of this amount is owed by just five per cent of the individuals, companies and organisations involved, so it can hardly be claimed that Greece is a nation of tax dodgers. On the other hand, it's true to say that most Greeks have a highly developed aversion to handing over any money at all to the state, but since politicians and government officials have been robbing the country blind for years, it's not that surprising that ordinary people say to themselves, 'Well, if that lot are all doing it, why shouldn't I?'

It's also worth mentioning that the vast majority of Greeks make a clear distinction between cheating the state and cheating other individuals. During one of our first olive harvests, for instance, we discovered that our local, family-run olive press had overpaid us by two hundred euros for the oil we'd produced, but when we told Dionysis, the thirty-year-old son, he said, 'No we haven't.'

'You have,' I said and showed him the paper with his own calculations on it and the two hundred euro error.

Even then, he wasn't convinced, and it took several more minutes to persuade him that we needed to pay him back the money. Unfortunately, I'd forgotten to bring the cash with me, so I went back to the press two days later to hand it over.

'But you already gave me the two hundred euros,' said Dionysis.

There then followed another debate about whether I'd

repaid the money or not, but eventually he accepted it with an air of scepticism that said, "Okay then, I'll take it if it'll make you happy, but I'm still not sure you're right".

Never before in my life had I had to argue quite so hard with somebody – twice – that I actually owed them money.

Despite the crippling austerity measures in Greece, the Greek people still retain their thoroughly deserved reputation for hospitality and generosity. After all, the very concept of Greek hospitality is enshrined in the language itself since the word *xénos* means both "stranger" and "guest". As for Greek generosity, here's just one example of the many that we've come across ourselves.

Besides running an olive press, Dionysis's family are farmers, and they have a regular stall at one of the local Sunday morning markets to sell their produce. Whenever we go, we always make a point of buying some fruit and veg from them, but even though Vasso, Dionysis's mother, only charges a pittance, she stills insists on giving us a carrier bag full of other stuff as a gift, thereby wiping out what little profit she would have made in the first place.

Even those who are no longer able to be as generous as they used to be in terms of buying drinks, giving gifts and so on are certainly generous with their time when it comes to helping someone out in an emergency. And not just in an emergency either. Not long ago, we needed to buy some tent pegs, and since there isn't anything that remotely resembles a camping/outdoor shop in Kyparissia, we decided that Taki's Aladdin's cave emporium would be the most likely source. Taki didn't have any, but another customer in the shop – a complete stranger – had overheard our conversation, and he said he knew a place not far away that might be able to help us. He then began to give us directions to the shop in question but broke off as soon as he noticed my blank expression.

'Come with me,' he said, and I followed him outside to his battered old moped.

'Hop on,' he said and then drove me about three hundred metres to the shop he had in mind, which unfortunately didn't have tent pegs either.

Vangelis (for such was his name) was profusely, and quite unnecessarily, apologetic about having wasted my time when he dropped me back at Taki's and bemoaned the fact that in a town like Kyparissia there wasn't a single shop where you could find tent pegs. However, in the spirit of the expression I've used a few times in this book already – in Greece, everything is difficult, but nothing is impossible – it wasn't long before we found a local metalworker who happily knocked us up a whole bunch of tent pegs for minimal expense.

Getting help from a total stranger without even having to ask for it is one of the many aspects of living in Greece that no longer takes us by surprise. After thirteen years, we're pretty much accustomed to how things are done here and the cultural differences, but it's not all been plain sailing since we upped sticks and burned our bridges back in the winter of 2003/4. [*Editor: I think you might be overdoing the metaphors here.*] It's certainly not been a constant bed of roses, and there have been plenty of thorns along the way. [*Editor: Careful now.*] I've mentioned several of these "thorns" during the course of this book, although, hopefully, I've also managed to convey many of the positive aspects of what it's like to be an expat in Greece, which far outweigh the negative.

But the one thing I doubt I'll ever get used to is having to buy things like rope and string by the kilo. And speaking of which, I hope you'll excuse me as I have to get to town now before the shops shut as I'm in urgent need of 0.37 kilos of string. At least, I think that's how much I need.

THE END

DEAR READER

Authors always appreciate reviews – especially if they're good ones of course – so I'd be eternally grateful if you could spare the time to write a few words about *A Kilo of String* on Amazon or anywhere else you can think of. It really can make a difference. Reviews also help other readers decide whether to buy a book or not, so you'll be doing them a service as well.

AND FINALLY...

Some of the material in *A Kilo of String* is loosely based on my podcast series of the same name. All episodes are free to listen to and download at:

https://rob-johnson.org.uk/podcasts/a-kilo-of-string/

I'm always interested to hear from my readers and listeners, so please do take a couple of minutes to contact me via my website at:

https://rob-johnson.org.uk/contact/

or email me at:

robjohnson@care4free.net

I look forward to hearing from you.

OTHER BOOKS BY ROB JOHNSON

LIFTING THE LID

(Book One in the 'Lifting the Lid' series)

There are some things people see in toilets that they wish they hadn't. What Trevor Hawkins sees might even cost him his life...

It was simply a matter of a broken flush, so how come he's suddenly a fugitive from a gang of psychopathic villains, a private detective, the police and MI5? 'Lifting the Lid' is a comic thriller with more twists and turns than an Escher-designed bobsleigh run.

"**A superb adventure-comedy.**" - Jennifer Reinoehl for *Readers' Favorite*

"**It's brilliant!**" - Samantha Coville for *SammytheBookworm.com*

"**The story is just so much FUN!**" - Joanne Armstrong for *Ingrid Hall Reviews*

HEADS YOU LOSE

(Book Two in the 'Lifting the Lid' series)

The assignment in Greece might have been the answer to Trevor and Sandra's problems except for one thing. Someone was trying to frame them for murder... with a watermelon.

Trevor and Sandra's detective agency is almost bankrupt when they take on the job of looking after the ageing Marcus Ingleby at his villa in Greece. It's easy money until someone tries to frame them for murder, and Ingleby gets a visit from two ex-cons and a police inspector from his murky past.

"A highly entertaining, well-constructed screwball comedy." - Keith Nixon for *Big Al's Books and Pals*

"Masterfully planned and executed... It tickled my funny bone in all the right places." - Joanne Armstrong for *Ingrid Hall Reviews*

Shortlisted for a Readers' Choice Award 2015 (*Big Al's Books and Pals*)

QUEST FOR THE HOLEY SNAIL

(A time travel comedy adventure)

WANTED: Gainful employment of an adventurous nature but without risk of personal physical harm. (Can supply own time travel machine if required.)

When Horace Tweed places an advertisement in a national magazine, the last thing he expects is to be commissioned to travel back through time in search of the long extinct Holey Snail.

But this isn't just any old snail. The *helix pertusa* is possessed of an extraordinary and highly desirable property, and Horace's quest leads him and his co-adventurers to Ancient Greece and a variety of near-death encounters with beings both mythological and not so mythological.

Meanwhile, Detective Chief Inspector Harper Collins has her hands full trying to track down a secret order of fundamentalist monks whom she suspects of committing a series of murders – the same monks who are determined to thwart Horace in his quest.

"Fans of Douglas Adams' *Hitchhikers' Guide to the Galaxy* will enjoy *Quest for the Holey Snail*." - *Awesome Indies*

"The author is a talented wordsmith with a penchant for Monty Python-esque humour... Overall, the writing is excellent." - Lynne Hinkey for *Underground Book Reviews*

"Not just another book about serial-killing monks who travel through time and wear Union Jack flip-flops." - *Unusual Footwear Monthly*

ABOUT THE AUTHOR

Since *A Kilo of String* is (mostly) autobiographical and if you've read it all the way through to here, you probably think there's not much more to know about me. Either that or you've heard enough about me already and you're really not that interested in finding out any more. However, because it seems almost compulsory these days to include an author biography somewhere in the book, here's mine...

I've written three novels so far, the most recent being a comedy time travel adventure called *Quest for the Holey Snail*. Prior to this, I published the first two books in my 'Lifting the Lid' comedy thriller series (*Lifting the Lid* and *Heads You Lose*).

I have written professionally for the theatre, and my career as a playwright began after having worked for several years as an administrator and publicist for touring theatre companies. Four of my plays were toured throughout the UK, but when public funding for non-commercial theatre virtually dried up overnight, I was forced into the world of "proper jobs" as my father liked to call them.

Some of these were less "proper" than others and included working in the towels and linens stockroom at Debenhams, as a fitter's mate in a perfume factory, a multi-drop delivery driver, and a motorcycle dispatch rider. I was actually sacked from the last of these jobs because, according to my boss, 'We could get a truck there quicker.'

Finally – and this will hardly come as a big surprise –

I live in Greece with my wife, Penny, five rescue dogs, two cats and four hundred and twenty olive trees. I'm currently working on a fourth novel and a couple of screenplays.

Right, that's probably more than enough about me, but if you're a glutton for punishment and would like any more information, please…

- visit my website at
  http://www.rob-johnson.org.uk
  (where you can also listen to my series of podcasts, which coincidentally is also called *A Kilo of String*);

- follow **@RobJohnson999** on Twitter;

- check out my Facebook author page at
  www.facebook.com/RobJohnsonAuthor

"LIFTING THE LID"
OPENING CHAPTERS

I hope you've enjoyed reading *A Kilo of String* and that you might be interested in reading one of my novels. To give you an idea what to expect, these are the opening chapters of *Lifting the Lid*, which is the first in my comedy thriller series.

LIFTING THE LID
CHAPTER ONE

Trevor stood with his back to the fireplace like some Victorian patriarch but without a scrap of the authority. Although the gas fire wasn't on, he rubbed his hands behind him as if to warm them. His mother sat in her usual chair by the window, staring blankly at the absence of activity in the street outside.

He knew exactly what her response would be. It was always the same when he told her anything about his life. Not that there was often much to tell, but this was different. This was a biggie. Almost as big as when he'd told her about Imelda's—

'It's of no concern to me.'

There we go. And now for the follow-on. Wait for it. Wait for it.

'I'm seventy-eight years old. Why should I care? I could be dead tomorrow.'

Trevor screwed up his face and mouthed the words of his mother's familiar mantra, but it became rapidly unscrewed again when she added, '…Like Imelda.'

'Don't,' he said. 'Just don't, okay?'

'No concern to me,' said the old woman with a barely perceptible shrug.

In the silence that followed, Trevor became aware of the ticking of the pendulum clock on the mantelpiece behind him. It had never been right since his father had died, so he checked his watch instead. 'You won't be… ' and he hesitated to say the word, ' … lonely?'

If his mother had had the energy or inclination to have laughed – derisively or otherwise – she would have done, but she settled for the next best option and grunted, 'Hmph.'

Trevor knew from experience that the intention was to pick away at his already tender guilt spot, and he looked around the room as if he were searching for the nearest escape route. His mother still referred to it as "the parlour", perhaps in a vain attempt to attach some kind of outmoded elegance to a room which, to Trevor's eye at least, was mildly shabby and darkly depressing even on the brightest of days. It was festooned with fading photographs of people who were long since dead, interspersed here and there with pictures of his more recently deceased brother and his very-much-alive sister. Of Trevor, there was only the one – an unframed snapshot of him and Imelda on their wedding day.

He became aware of the clock once again and cleared his throat. 'So… er… I'll be away then.'

This time, the shrug was accompanied by the slightest tilt of the head. 'No concern to me,' she said.

Again, he glanced at his watch. 'It's just that I have to—'

'Oh get on if you're going.'

Trevor stepped forward and, picking up his crash

helmet from the table next to his mother, kissed her perfunctorily on the back of the head. For the first time, she turned – not quite to face him, but turned nevertheless.

'Still got that silly little moped then,' she said, repeating the comment she'd made when he had first arrived less than an hour before.

'Scooter, mother. It's a scooter. – Anyway, how could I afford anything else?' He was thankful she couldn't see the sudden redness in his cheeks or she would have instantly realised that he was lying.

He kissed her again in the same spot, and this time she seemed to squirm uncomfortably. For a moment, he followed her line of vision to the outside world. – Nothing. He tapped his helmet a couple of times, then turned and walked towards the door. As he closed it behind him, he could just make out the words: 'Your brother wouldn't have gone.'

Out in the street, he strapped on his helmet and straddled the ageing Vespa, eventually coaxing the engine into something that resembled life. He took a last look at the window where his mother sat and thought he saw the twitch of a lace curtain falling back into place.

'Oh sod it,' he said aloud and let out the clutch.

At the end of the road, he turned right and stopped almost immediately behind a parked camper van. Dismounting the Vespa and still holding the handlebars, he kicked out the side stand and was about to lean it to rest when he decided that some kind of symbolic gesture was called for. Instead of inclining the scooter to a semi-upright position, he looked down at the rust-ridden old machine, tilted it marginally in the opposite direction and let go. With the gratingly inharmonious sound of metal on tarmac, the Vespa crashed to the ground and twitched a few times before rattling itself into submission. Trevor took in the paltry death throes and allowed himself a smirk of satisfaction.

Pulling a set of keys from his pocket, he kissed it lightly and walked round to the driver's door of the van. The moment he turned the key in the lock, a lean-looking black and tan mongrel leapt from its sleeping position on the back seat and hurled itself towards the sound. By the time Trevor had opened the door, the dog was standing on the driver's seat, frantically wagging its tail and barking hysterically.

'Hey, Milly. Wasn't long, was I?' said Trevor, taking the dog's head between both hands and rocking it gently from side to side. 'Over you get then.'

Milly simply stared back at him, no longer barking but still wagging her tail excitedly.

'Go on. Get over.' Trevor repeated the command and, with a gentle push, encouraged her to jump across to the passenger seat. Then he climbed in and settled himself behind the steering wheel. 'Right then,' he said, rubbing his palms around its full circumference. 'Let's get this show on the road.'

LIFTING THE LID
CHAPTER TWO

The lift was dead. The grey-haired guy in the expensive suit wasn't, but he looked like he was. Lenny had him pinned against the wall by leaning his back into him as hard as he could to keep him upright – no mean achievement since, although built like a whippet on steroids, Lenny was little more than five feet in height and well into his fifties.

'Come on, Carrot,' he said. 'What you messin' about at?'

Carrot – so called because of his ill-fitting and very obvious ginger toupee – jabbed at the lift button for the umpteenth time. 'Lift's not working. We'll have to use the stairs.'

'You kidding me? With this lard-arse?'

'So we just leave him here, do we?'

Lenny's heavily lined features contorted into a grimace. 'How many flights?'

'Dunno. Couple maybe?'

'Jesus,' said Lenny, taking a step forward.

The laws of gravity instantly came into play, and the Suit slid inexorably down the wall and ended up in a sitting position, his head lolled to one side and his jacket bunched up around his ears. Not for the first time, Carrot wondered why he'd been paired up with a dipshit like Lenny and even why the whining little git had been put on this job at all.

'Well you'll have to take the top half then,' Lenny said. 'Back's playing me up.'

Carrot snorted. Here we go again, he thought. The old racing injury ploy.

Lenny pulled himself up to his full inconsiderable height and shot him a glare. 'And what's that supposed to mean? You know bloody well about my old racing injury.'

'Doesn't everyone?' said Carrot.

Although Lenny's stature – or lack of it – gave a certain amount of credibility to his countless stories about when he used to be a top-flight steeplechase jockey, nobody in the racing business ever seemed to have heard of him. It was certainly true that he knew pretty much everything there was to know about the Sport of Kings, and most of his tales of the turf had a ring of authenticity about them, so he must have been involved in some way or other but more likely as a stable lad than a jockey. Hardly anyone bothered to doubt him to his face though, probably because his vicious temper was legendary and so was his ability with both his fists and his feet. For a little guy, he could be more than handy when it came to a scrap.

He looked like he was spoiling for one right now, so Carrot diverted his attention back to the Suit.

'Grab his ankles then,' he said and manoeuvred the man's upper body forward so he could get a firm grip under his armpits from behind.

Halfway up the first flight of concrete stairs, Lenny announced that he'd have to have a rest. Even though Carrot was doing most of the work, he decided not to antagonise him and eased his end of the body down onto the steps. Truth be told, he could do with a short break himself. He was already sweating like a pig and, besides, he needed at least one hand free to push his toupee back from in front of his eyes.

Lenny leaned back against the iron handrail and started to roll a cigarette.

Carrot's jaw dropped. 'Lenny?'

'Yeah?'

'What you doing?'

'Er…' Lenny looked down at his half completed cigarette and then back at Carrot. 'Rollin' a fag?'

His expression and tone of voice rendered the addition of a "duh" utterly redundant.

'We're not in the removal business, you know.' Carrot nodded towards the Suit. 'This isn't some bloody wardrobe we're delivering.'

Lenny ignored him and lit up. He took a long drag and blew a couple of smoke rings. Putting the cigarette to his lips for a second time, he was about to take another draw when he hesitated and began to sniff the air. 'What's that smell?'

'Er… smoke?' Two can play the "duh" game, thought Carrot.

'It's like…' Lenny's nose twitched a few more times and then puckered with distaste. 'Ugh, it's piss.'

'Dumps like this always stink of piss.'

'No, it's more…' Lenny carried on sniffing, his eyes ranging around to try to identify the source of the smell. 'Oh Jesus, it's him.'

Carrot looked in the direction he was pointing and, sure enough, the dark stain which covered the Suit's groin area was clearly visible despite the charcoal grey of the trousers. 'Oh for f—'

'Bugger's wet 'imself.'

'I can see that.'

Lenny took a pull on his cigarette. 'Fear probably.'

'Don't be a prat. The man's out cold. He doesn't know if it's Christmas Day or Tuesday.'

'Maybe it's like when somebody has their leg cut off – or their arm. They reckon you can still feel it even though it's not there any more.'

Carrot stared at him, unable to discern any logical

connection between amputation and pissing your pants.

'You know,' Lenny continued, apparently aware that further explanation was necessary. 'It's like your subconscious, or whatever, doing stuff behind your back without you realising.'

'I think it's far more likely it's a side effect of the stuff we injected him with.'

'Could be,' said Lenny, and he took a last drag on his cigarette before lobbing it over his shoulder into the stairwell.

'Ready now?' Carrot made no attempt to disguise the sarcasm in his tone.

'I'm not taking the feet this time though. My face'll be right in his piss.'

Carrot squeezed his eyes shut and counted to three. 'You want to swap?'

'Not necessarily. We could try taking an arm each.'

Because of the substantial difference in their heights, Carrot knew that this meant he would be taking most of the weight again, but he also realised there was no point in arguing. The priority was to get the guy up the stairs and into the flat before somebody spotted them.

LIFTING THE LID
CHAPTER THREE

The time wandered by, and the miles slid comfortably under the tyres at a steady fifty-five. Battered though it was, the converted Volkswagen Transporter was only twelve years old and could have gone faster, but Trevor was in no particular hurry. He was enjoying the ride, happy to be away and with the road stretching before him to an unknown destination. Milly seemed equally contented and alternated between sitting upright on the passenger seat, staring fixedly ahead, and curling up to sleep in the back.

It was Trevor's first real trip in the camper, and he liked the idea of having no fixed itinerary. After all, he reasoned, wasn't that the whole point of having one of these things?

To say that he had bought it on a whim would have been a gross distortion of the truth. Trevor didn't really do whims. His idea of an impulsive action was to buy an item that wasn't on his list when he did his weekly shop at the local supermarket. Even then, there would have to be a pretty convincing argument in favour of dropping the quarter-pound packet of frozen peas, or whatever it might be, into his trolley. Half price or two-for-one were minimum requirements.

The camper van hadn't fulfilled either of these criteria, and to begin with, he'd toyed with the idea of a motorbike. Something a bit flash, like a Harley. He'd have needed a halfway decent tent of course. A simple bedroll and sleeping out under the stars were all very well in Arizona or wherever but totally inadequate over here – unless you were one of those rufty-tufty outdoor survival types with an unnatural fixation about the SAS. He'd never understood the attraction of deliberately putting yourself in a situation where it was more than likely you would either starve or freeze to death or be attacked by a large carnivore or stung by something so venomous you'd have seconds to live unless you applied the appropriate antidote in time or got your best friend to suck out the poison. No, Scottish midges were about as much as he was prepared to tolerate, but even then he'd make damn sure he had a plentiful supply of insect repellent with him.

A hermetically sealable tent and a good thick sleeping bag would be indispensable as far as Trevor was concerned and, if space permitted on the Harley, an airbed – preferably with a pump which operated off the bike's battery. It had all started to make perfect sense until a small problem finally occurred to him. What about Milly? She was too big to ride in a rucksack on his back, and as for the only other possible option, the very idea of a Harley with a sidecar made him squirm with embarrassment.

A car was far too ordinary for his purposes, so a camper van had seemed to be the next best thing if he couldn't have a Harley. It still had a kind of "just hit the open road and go where it takes you" feel to it, and he'd once read a book by John Steinbeck where he set off to rediscover America in a camper with an enormous poodle called Charley.

The whole decision-making process had taken months of what Imelda would have called "anally retentive faffing", but which Trevor preferred to consider as an essential prerequisite to "getting it right". In his defence, he would have argued that it wasn't just about buying a van. There had been much greater life choices involved, such as whether to pack in his job at Dreamhome Megastores.

As it turned out, that particular decision had almost made itself for him. The company was in a bit of financial bother and was having to make cutbacks, so he and several of his colleagues had been offered voluntary redundancy. Although not exactly generous, the severance package was certainly tempting enough to cause Trevor a run of sleepless nights. But it wasn't until his annual staff appraisal that he'd finally made up his mind.

He had sat across the desk from the store manager and studied the thin wisps of hair on top of the man's head while he read out a litany of shortcomings and misdemeanours from the form in front of him.

'This simply won't do, Trevor. Really it won't,' Mr Webber had said, finally looking up and removing his glasses. 'I mean, there have been more customer complaints about you than any other member of staff.'

'I don't know why. I'm always polite. Always try and give advice whenever I—'

'But that's exactly the problem, Trevor. More often than not, the complaints are *about* your advice. We've had more goods returned because of you than… than…' The manager had slumped back in his chair. 'Good God, man, have you learned nothing about home maintenance and improvement in all the… What is it? Fourteen years since you've been here?'

'Fifteen.' And in all those long years, he'd never once heard Webber use the phrase "do-it-yourself", let alone its dreaded acronym.

'Quite honestly, I'm at a loss as to know what to—'

This time, it was Trevor who had interrupted. He couldn't be sure that he was about to be sacked, but he'd already had his quota of verbal and written warnings and thought he'd get in first with: 'About this voluntary redundancy thing...'

And that was that. Decision made and not a bad little payout. Added to what he'd squirreled away over the last couple of years or so, he could buy the van and still have enough left to live on for a few months as long as he was careful. He'd have to look for another job when the money did run out of course, but he was determined not to worry about that until the time came. At least, he was determined to *try* not to worry about it.

'What the hell, eh, Milly? This is *it*,' he said and shoved a tape into the cassette player.

He caught sight of the dog in the rear-view mirror. She briefly raised an eyebrow when the opening bars of Steppenwolf's *Born to be Wild* bellowed from the speakers above her head. Then she went back to sleep.

Trevor tapped the steering wheel almost in time with the music and hummed along when the lyrics kicked in. A song about hitting the open road and just seeing where it took you seemed particularly appropriate for the occasion, and when it got to the chorus, he'd begun to lose all sense of inhibition and joined in at the top of his voice.

Moments later, the van's engine spluttered and then abruptly died.

LIFTING THE LID
CHAPTER FOUR

Carrot and Lenny hauled the Suit to his feet and, with an arm slung around each of their shoulders, half carried and half dragged him up to the first floor landing. As Carrot had predicted, Lenny's contribution amounted to little more than providing a largely ineffectual counterbalance, and by the time they'd lurched and staggered to the top of the second flight of steps, every muscle in his neck and back was screaming at him to stop whatever he was doing.

'I'm gonna have to... have a break for a minute,' he said, fighting for breath as he altered his grip and lowered the Suit to the ground.

'Come on, mate. We're nearly there now,' said Lenny, but his words of encouragement were meaningless, given that he did nothing to prevent the Suit's descent.

Carrot groaned as he sat him down against the frame of the fire door and so did the Suit.

''Ang on a sec. He's not coming round, is he?' Lenny squatted like a jockey at the start gate and brought his face to within a few inches of the Suit's. 'He is, you know.'

The muscles in Carrot's back grumbled as he crouched down to take a closer look and spotted the faintest flicker of the eyelids.

'You can't have given him enough,' said Lenny.

'What?'

'The injection.'

'Yeah, stupid me,' said Carrot, slapping his palm against his forehead. 'I should've allowed extra time for all your fag breaks.'

Even though he resented Lenny's accusation, he'd worked with him on several other jobs and was used to getting the blame when things went wrong. Not that this was surprising since Lenny always avoided making any of the decisions, so any cockups were never his fault.

'We'll have to give him another shot,' said Lenny.

"We" meaning "you", Carrot thought and shook his head. 'Stuff's still in the van.'

'Jesus, man. What you leave it there for?'

Carrot bit his lip, aware from his peripheral vision that Lenny was staring at him, but he had no intention of shifting his focus to make eye contact. The Suit's eyelids were twitching more rapidly now and occasionally parted to reveal two narrow slits of yellowish white. Maybe the guy was just dreaming, but it was two hours or more since they'd given him the shot, so—

'Better bop him one, I reckon,' said Lenny.

It was Carrot's turn to stare at Lenny. 'Bop him one?'

'Yeah, you know…' He mimed hitting the Suit over the head with some blunt instrument or other and made a "click" sound with his tongue. 'Right on the noggin.'

Carrot continued to hold him in his gaze while he pondered which nineteen-fifties comedian Lenny reminded him of, but he was shaken from his musing by a strange moaning sound. The Suit's eyes were almost half open now.

END OF FIRST FOUR CHAPTERS OF 'LIFTING THE LID'

To read on, please go to:
http://viewbook.at/Lifting_the_Lid

Made in the USA
Coppell, TX
22 November 2021